The Theory of General Value
– Economics, Business, Decision-Making –

Sergey K. Aityan
Alexey K. Ivanov-Schitz

Copyright © 2022
Sergey K. Aityan and Alexey K. Ivanov-Schitz
All rights reserved.
KDP Amazon
ISBN: 979-8844045660

Preface

This book introduces the concept of general value according to which value has two additive components—monetary and nonmonetary. The nonmonetary component reflects individual perception of value unrelated to the monetary part of it. The fundamental difference between the concept of general value and the conventional concept of value is in the expansion of the concept from monetary only to a more general concept by adding a distinct nonmonetary component.

The book introduces the principle of maximization of general value. that states that in every action or transaction, the general value for each participant should increase. Each decision maker always tries to maximize his/her general value that becomes the driving force for each decision, trading, or action. This principle lays the foundation for value-based quantitative decision-making. To make a decision, an individual needs to assess a difference of general values before and after the action or transaction.

The major methodological challenge in the theory of general value was related to measurement of the nonmonetary component of general value. This challenge was successfully resolved by applying the approach of indifferent point, which is the situation, when the difference of monetary components of value of two choices is balanced off by the difference of nonmonetary components of value. This situation constitutes the point of indifferent choices for the individual. At this point the difference of the nonmonetary values for a choice is equal to the difference of the monetary components with the opposite sign.

The theory of general value has been successfully applied to various areas of business and economics explaining and optimizing economic activities, which could not be explained or optimized without such an approach. Maximization of net present general value is a generalized principal goal of any business, organization, regardless either it is for-profit or not-for-profit/nonprofit, or even an individual. Such an approach eliminates existing uncertainty in formulating principal strategic goals beyond pure monetary approach. The approach of general value has been applied and illustrated for the choice of job, consumer decisions on purchasing products and services. Business competitive strategies and funds migrations between industries have found the better explanation with the application of the concept of general value.

The theory of general value provides a quantitative approach to the theory of value by separating the monetary and nonmonetary components of value. The nonmonetary component of value accounts for psychological factors and biases in contrast to the monetary component in trading and decision making.

The separation of monetary and nonmonetary components of value allows for a clear and measurable account for nonmonetary factors in decision making. Nonmonetary factors may go far beyond economic incentives and account for all psychological factors and biases, which can be distinctly measured, analyzed, and taken into account.

The book contains a a lot of real-world case studies and examples that help understand the concept of general value and its applicability for solving practical problems in business and economics. The concept of general value is easily extendable to other human activities and decision-making.

Sergey K. Aityan, DSc, PhD, Professor

Table of Contents (Brief)

1 The Notion of Value in Economics 1
2 Introducing General Value 13
3 Measuring the Nonmonetary Component of Value 33
4 Measuring Nonmonetary Value of Jobs in San Francisco Bay Area 55
5 Measuring Nonmonetary Value of Jobs in Europe 87
6 Measuring Nonmonetary Value of Consumer Products 95
7 Measuring Nonmonetary Value of Services 107
8 Transaction Power and Efficiency 117
9 Trading a Paper Clip for a Single Family Home 129
10 Competitive Strategy 141
11 Market Share Analysis 153
12 Explanatory and Predictive Power of General Value 161
Bibliography 167

Table of Contents (Detailed)

1 **The Notion of Value in Economics** 1
   1.1 Price and Value 1
   1.2 Major Theories of Value 3
   1.3 A Missing Link 9
   1.4 The Need for Distinction between Monetary and Nonmonetary Values 10

2 **Introducing General Value** 13
   2.1 Monetary and Nonmonetary Components of Value 13
   2.2 Measuring General Value 14
   2.3 Principle of Increasing General Value 17
   2.4 Special Cases and Examples 18
   2.5 Isovalue 26
   2.6 Business Analysis 27
   2.7 Difference between General Value and Utility 29
   2.8 Summarizing the Concept of General Value 30

3 **Measuring the Nonmonetary Component of Value** 33
   3.1 Units for Measuring Nonmonetary Value 33
   3.2 The Indifference Point 34
   3.3 General Value of Jobs 35
   3.4 General Value in Purchasing Decision 40
   3.5 Methodology of Measuring Nonmonetary Values 44
   3.6 Survey Method for Finding the Indifference Point..... 45
   3.7 The Survey for Job Selection 45
   3.8 The Survey for Purchasing Decision 49
   3.9 Nonmonetary Values as Perceptual Bias 52

4 **Measuring Nonmonetary Value of Jobs in San Francisco Bay Area** 55
   4.1 Survey Domain and Sampling 55
   4.2 The Survey among Business Students of Lincoln University, Oakland, CA 56
   4.3 The Survey among Taxi Drivers in the Berkeley-Oakland-San Francisco Area 63
   4.4 Survey among Construction Workers in Berkeley-Oakland-San Francisco Area 70
   4.5 Survey among Restaurant Waiters 77
   4.6 Analysis of the Results by all Group of Respondents 83
   4.7 Discussion on the Job Selection Survey 85

5	**Measuring Nonmonetary Value of Jobs in Europe**	**87**
	5.1 The Surveys on Job Selection in Europe	87
	5.2 The Survey on Nonmonetary Value of Jobs in Germany	87
	5.3 The Survey on Nonmonetary Value of Jobs in Russia	91
6	**Measuring Nonmonetary Value of Consumer Products**	**95**
	6.1 General Value in Buying Decisions	95
	6.2 The Survey Domain and Sampling	96
	6.3 Measuring Nonmonetary Values of Smartphones	97
	6.4 Measuring the Nonmonetary Value of the *Christian Louboutin* Brand in Russia	101
	6.5 Measuring the Nonmonetary Value of the *Mazda* Car Brand in Russia	103
7	**Measuring Nonmonetary Value of Services**	**107**
	7.1 General Value in Service Purchasing Decisions	107
	7.2 Measuring the Nonmonetary Value of the *Starbucks* Coffee Brand in Germany	108
	7.3 Measuring the Nonmonetary Value of Specialized Car Services in Russia	111
	7.4 Measuring the Nonmonetary Value of Airlines in Russia	113
8	**Transaction Power and Efficiency**	**117**
	8.1 Increasing General Value	117
	8.2 Transaction Power and Efficiency	119
	8.3 Relative Addedd General Value	121
	8.4 Efficiency of Purely Monetary Transactions	122
	8.5 Efficiency of Purely Nonmonetary Transactions	123
	8.6 Efficiency of Transactions with Mixed Components	124
	8.7 Circulation of General Values versus Economic Factors	126
9	**Trading a Paper Clip for a Single Family Home**	**129**
	9.1 From a Paper Clip to a Single Family House	129
	9.2 A Barter Chain Trader versus a Consumer	130
	9.3 Marginal Value for the Trader and the Consumer	134
	9.4 The Chain of Barter Trades to Grow Monetary Value	135
	9.5 From a Paper Clip to a Single-Family Home	137

9.6 Using Nonmonetary Value for Growing
Monetary Profit 139
10 Competitive Strategy 141
10.1 General Value of Products to Purchase 141
10.2 Buying Decision without Additional Constrains 142
10.3 Sales of Computer Monitors as an Example of
Competitive Power 146
10.4 Buying Decisions under Monetary and
Nonmonetary Constrains 150
11 Market Share Analysis 153
11.1 Analogy with Physics 153
11.2 Summarizing the Concept of General Value 154
11.3 Market Share Analysis as Boltzmann Distribution... 154
11.4 Conclusions on Market Share 159
**12 Explanatory and Predictive Power of General
Value 161**
12.1 A Brief Summary of the Theory of General Value... 161
12.2 The Explanatory Power of the Theory of General
Value 162
12.3 The Principal Strategic Goal of a Company 164
12.4 Market Share Analysis and Prediction 165
12.5 Cross-Industry Capital Flows Analysis and
Prediction 165
Bibliography 167

1 The Notion of Value in Economics

1.1 Price and Value

Most economic theories were built on the notion of money and price. Traditionally, the notion of value in economics refers to money. Market demand and supply, market equilibrium, and other economic concepts typically refer to money too. Such an approach creates certain "blind spots" and leads to "missing links" in economic theories. For example, it is commonly agreed that the general long-term strategic goal of a for-profit firm in a free-market economy is the maximization of the wealth of its owners. This translates into maximization of the net present value of the firm where term "value" refers to money.

It would be a mistake to define the major long-term strategic goal of a firm as profit maximization. Such a goal is quite nearsighted and could lead to wrong decisions. Profit maximization is an operational goal that can be considered a tactical goal Though profit and value are related, they are not directly tied together. For example, Tesla, Inc. which was founded in 2003 and sold its first electric car "Roadster" in 2009, has been a high value company as of its market capitalization though it was losing significant amounts of money till 2019 and first time showed annual profit only in 2020. Nevertheless, even losing money and being a relatively small automaker, Tesla's market capitalization has been significantly higher than capitalization of giant automakers such as Toyota, GM, and Volkswagen. Thus, the principal strategic goal of any commercial firm is maximization of its net present value.

However, when the same question about the primary goal is asked about not-for-profit organizations, an accurate and measurable answer is no longer available. Even in case of a for-profit firm, such a primary goal as maximization of the net present value of the firm looks extremely money-centric and it seems that the firm should not do anything that may not increase its monetary value because its goal is considered only from the perspective of money. This leaves no room in this approach for charity or any free services to individuals or community which reduce the monetary value of the firm.

Market models describe idealized markets with certain parameters. On the other hand, real-world markets are more diverse and their variety may not fit the constraints of idealized models. It is unfeasible to develop a model for each particular real-world market. For this reason, market models are supposed to serve reference points to approximate the behavior of the real-world markets. For example, the model of perfectly competitive market is an abstraction, but such idealized markets do not exist in the real world in its pure form. However, some markets are quite close to the perfectly competitive market model though somehow deviate from it. Among real-world markets farmers market is one of the closest to the model of perfect competition. According to the model of perfect competition, sellers and buyers in such a market are small enough not to influence the market equilibrium and all sellers offer uniform products with no differentiation, so buying decisions are based exclusively on price. Therefore, firms in a perfectly competitive market are price takers and have to charge a uniform price. However, products or services offered by any real-world firm are different—maybe slightly different but different—from products or services of other firms on the same market and for this reason may be sold at slightly different prices. For this reason, the model of perfect competition works only for theoretically perfectly competitive firms and cannot be extended to a near-perfectly competitive markets without losing it meaning. Thus, the model of a perfectly competitive market may become practically unusable because real-world firms cannot use its conclusions for pricing decision because every product of each firm may show slight differentiation.

Decisions on pricing strategies in different markets, analysis of consumer behavior, assessment of balance and equilibrium between different markets, and many other problems in economics which are pursued with the traditional price-quantity approach face significant challenges and lack clarity.

1.2 Major Theories of Value

The notion of value plays the central role in economics. Generations of economists have developed the appropriate theories trying to define and better understand the notion of value and economic implications from it. The term "theory of value" refers to all such theories rather than to a certain specific approach in theory of value. Value is typically understood as an exchange measure and sometimes simply a price of goods and services. The variety of the theories of value can be divided into two major categories:

- Intrinsic or objective theories
- Subjective theories

Intrinsic theories are based on the classical theory of value that, following Adam Smith (1776) and David Ricardo (1817), suggest that prices of goods and services come from objective parameters, say, production cost rather than from subjective considerations (Hollander, 1979). Classical economics follows the labor theory of value. On the other hand, subjective theories presume that price is determined by subjective and perceptual judgments based on satisfaction of consumer desires, utility of the appropriate products or services, and the limitations in their supply. Subjective theories in neoclassical economics originated from marginalism, introduced independently by William Jevons (1879), Carl Menger (1871), and Leon Walras (1874, 1877) in the 70s of nineteenth century. Marginalism suggests that value of a good or service is determined by an additional satisfaction (marginal utility) from the most recently added unit of the good or service. Thus, value represents the most recent rate of exchange. The concept of marginal utility can be easily illustrated with a diamond-water paradox which was first introduced in 1880s. In normal conditions water has a much higher practical utility for a human than diamonds but diamonds have a higher value because marginal utility of a diamond is much higher than a marginal utility of water (Rhoads, 2007). However, value of water in case of water shortage may significantly exceed the value of diamonds in terms of marginal utility because humans cannot survive without water.

Marginalism laid foundations for neoclassical economics in late nineteenth century that related market demand, supply, and equilibrium to rationality of individuals to maximize their profits or utility. The principles of neoclassical economics have become the major platform for majority of economic theories of the twentieth century. The major criticism of neoclassical approach in economics relates to the presumption of the exclusively rational behavior of market participants. A comprehensive review of neoclassical economics and its view on the concept of value is provided in recent publications (Kahn, 1979; McKenzie &Tullock, 1981; Pollis & Koslin, 1962).

1.2.1 Objective Theories: Classical Economics

Intrinsic theories attempt to define value objectively with human perception taken out of picture. These theories are based on classical economics that defines value as labor involved in the production of goods or rendering services (Smith, 1776; Ricardo, 1817). *Labor value* measures the quantity of labor put in the product. Marx[1] (1867) divided value into two categories, *use value* and *exchange value*. Use value represents the utility of a product or a service or the need for the product or service. Exchange value measures the ability of products or services to exchange in certain proportions and hence represents price. According to the precepts of classical and Marxian economics, use value is impossible to measure and therefore, the only measurable is exchange value that is measured by the labor involved in the production of a good of rendering a service. Adam Smith (1776) wrote, - "It was not by gold or by silver, but by labor, that all the

---

[1] Karl Marx did not identify himself as a classical economist but actually supported the labor theory of value in classical economics.

wealth of the world was originally purchased; and its value, to those who possess it, and who want to exchange it for some new productions, is precisely equal to the quantity of labor which it can enable them to purchase or command." Thus, classical economics did not address the relationship between the use value and exchange value and stayed on the purely objective grounds of labor theory of value.

1.2.2 Subjective Theories: Neoclassical Economics

Marginalism laid foundations for neoclassical economics in the late nineteenth century. Hermann Gossen (1854), a Prussian economist, was the first who introduced a general approach to marginal utility though many other economists by that time had already elaborated on various specific aspects of value in terms of human perception.

Subjective theories originated from marginalism were independently developed by Hermann Gossen (1854), William Jevons in 1879 (Jevons, 2010), Carl Menger in 1871 (Menger, 2007), and Leon Walras in 1874 and 1877 (Walras, 2010) in the second part of the nineteenth century. Subjective theories define value in terms of human perception of satisfaction with goods or services and limitations in their supply. Menger argued that value is essentially subjective. The concept of utility as a measure of satisfaction was introduced in neoclassical economics to measure value, thus replacing the objective concept of value in classical economics with the purely subjective approach. It is important to emphasize that by replacing the labor approach in the definition of value in classical economics with the perceptual approach in neoclassical economics has denoted a fundamental shift in the view on value from producers to consumers.

Marginalism suggests that value of a good or a service is determined by an additional satisfaction (marginal utility) from the most recently added unit of the good or service. The more quantity of something you have, the less quantity of something else you would be willing to give up for one additional unit of it. This law is referred to as a law of diminishing marginal utility. Thus, value represents the most recent rate of exchange. The concept of marginal utility and the law of diminishing marginal utility can be easily illustrated with a diamond-water paradox which was first introduced in 1880s. Water under normal circumstances has a much higher practical utility for a human, than diamonds, but diamonds have a higher value because marginal utility of diamonds is much higher than a marginal utility of water (Rhoads, 2007). However, value of water in case of water shortage may significantly exceed the value of diamonds in terms of marginal utility because humans cannot survive without water.

The principles of neoclassical economics have become the major platform for majority of economic theories of the twentieth century. The major criticism of neoclassical approach in economics relates to the presumption of the exclusively rational behavior of market participants. A comprehensive review of neoclassical economics and its view on the concept of value is widely available in the literature (Kahn, 1979; McKenzie & Tullock, 1981; Pollis & Koslin, 1962).

The next step in the development of neoclassical concepts in economics was related to Alfred Marshall (1890), a British economist, who developed the well-known supply and demand chart, that forms market equilibrium and establishes the relationship between quantity and price in regard to supply and demand. However, Marshall did not distinguish between price and value and presumed, that all market participants possess full information about the related market conditions.

Samuelson and Nordhaus (2004) wrote, - "... but you should definitively resist the idea that utility is a psychological function or feeling that can be observed or measured. Rather, utility is a scientific construct that economists use to understand how rational consumers divide their limited resources among commodities that provide them with satisfaction."

Let's apply the neoclassical concept of value to employment, compensation, and the impact of non-financial factors on job selection decisions. There are many other factors beyond financial compensation that impact the job selection decisions such as job prestige, professional challenges, work environment, proximity to the residence. These factors contribute to the value of the job in the perception of an employee or a job candidate. It is evident, that less prestigious jobs should offer a higher financial compensation to equalize the value of the job in the perception of employees or job candidates. This issue was addressed in the theory of equalizing differences (Brown, 1980; Rosen, 1983). The theory attempted to explain why employees in similar positions receive different compensations in different geographic locations. The results of this analysis showed that employees receive additional compensation for adverse work conditions. However, Rosen made a simplifying assumption about the uniformity of individual preferences that ignores the fact that employees may prefer different activities under all equal conditions. Challenges of heterogeneous models of human capital have been recently addressed in the literature (Blackaby & Murphy, 1995; Han & Yamaguchi, 2015).

Gary Becker (1968) tried to apply the neoclassical utility approach to the analysis of criminal behavior. However, the model assumed rational behavior of criminals though most of the time rational factors do not play a decisive role.

1.2.3 Neoclassical Theories and Schools

Among many directions in economics, neoclassical Austrian and Chicago schools of economics made significant contributions to the development of the modern theory of value. The Austrian school traces its origin to late nineteenth century and is associated with such names as Friedrich von Wieser (1889, 2012), Carl Menger (1871), Eugen von Böhm-Bawerk (1890), and Ludwig von Mises (1912). Friedrich von Wieser in his famous book "Natural Value" (1889a, 1889b) introduced the imputation theory. The imputation theory argues that the price of output determines the prices of input factors. This approach is inverse to the classical (Smith, 1776; Ricardo, 1817; Hollander, 1979; Marx, 1867) labor approach by which prices of production inputs determine the price of the output. Carl Menger (1871) argued that there was always a difference of values of present goods and future goods of equal quality, quantity, and form. According to Böhm-Bawerk (1890) there are three reasons for this difference of values: (a) in a growing economy, the supply of goods will grow with time, so it will always be higher in the future than at the present time; (b) people normally underestimate their future needs due to carelessness and shortsightedness; (c) and entrepreneurs prefer to produce with inputs currently available rather than postpone their production to wait until the inputs become available in the future. A comprehensive review of the cornerstones of the Austrian school of economics is presented by Simon Bilo (2005).

The Chicago school of economics can be traced back to the Milton Friedman's paper "Essays in Positive Economics" (Friedman, 1953). Though both Austrian and Chicago schools agree on most major concepts of free market and capitalism, the Chicago school is known for its focus on monetarism and emphasizes the role of government in controlling amount of money in circulation. This implies that national output is affected by money supply. The Chicago school, built with a strong overlap between law and economics, has considered economic processes to be tightly related to other aspects of the society (Baker, 2003) and believed macroeconomics to be tightly related to microeconomics (Lucas, 1988). According to Ronald Coase (1937) firms are formed to reduce their costs by producing goods or rendering services internally rather than purchasing them on the market. The major commonalities and differences between the Austrian and Chicago schools and their concepts of value are clearly presented and discussed in the review published by Ludwig von Mises Institute (Murphy, 2011).

1.2.4 Subjective Theories: Behavioral Economics

Neoclassical economics has built the major foundation for economic theories of twentieth century and helped better understand economic processes and relationships. However, the neoclassical approach presumed all participants of the market to be perfectly rational and analytic. Such a quite strong presumption does not actually reflect the way how humans actually make their decisions and act. Humans in their decision-making, mostly rely on habits, customs, beliefs, recommendations, or even on mimicking or imitating others rather than on shear rationality. This issue has been brought up for discussion by many authors for a long time.

It would be quite unrealistic to expect humans to be perfectly rational in their judgments and choices. Herbert Simon (1955, 1972) brought this issue up as the major criticism of the neoclassical economic approaches and models. He suggested that market participant have ***bounded rationality.*** Humans tend to act suboptimally and irrationally by using rules of thumb, hopes, and beliefs rather than accurate calculations.

Finally, a new direction in the economics was formed by closely tying up economics with human psychology and behavioral patterns All this gave rise of a new approach called ***behavioral economics*** (Simon, 1972; Kahneman & Tversky, 1979, 2000; Kahneman et al, 1982; Kahneman, 2011). According to this approach, human psychology and behavioral patterns play the major role in making judgments, choices, and decisions.

1.3   A Missing Link

Typically, fiat money, may have none or a very low commodity value but is commonly accepted only because of explicit or implicit common perception of money as value. However, money is not the only value and there are other values of a nonmonetary nature, which are specific to an individual, or a community, or a country, or to the entire mankind. Such nonmonetary values are completely subjective and given consideration at a time of choice, decision on action or transaction in addition to the monetary values. Though certain considerations on subjective perception of value have been given in the neoclassical economics, most discussions were focused on the perception of money and price. The notion of utility was introduced in neoclassical economics to account for perception of money but this attempt fell short of perception of nonmonetary values (Schulak & Unterkofler, 2011; Skousen, 2005; Gale & Swire, 2006).

The approach of compensating variations was introduced by Hicks (1939) as a measure of utility change in terms of additional money an individual needs to compensate for a change in price or product quality to keep the same level of satisfaction. With this approach consumer's surplus can be used as a welfare measure (Chipman & Moore, 1980). The theory of hedonic prices (Rosen, 1974) addresses the spatial equilibrium for differentiated product in which the entire set of implicit prices guides both consumers and producers locational decisions in characteristics space. This theory utilizes the hedonic hypothesis that goods are valued for their utility-bearing attributes or characteristics on the base is of the theory of equalizing differences. The theory of compensating differences has addressed the changes in utility with price but still was confined within the concept of monetary utility.

The theory of equalizing differences (Brown, 1980; Rosen, 1986) made a step towards a separation of monetary and nonmonetary perception in labor market stated that "workers receive compensating wage premiums when they accept jobs with undesirable nonwage characteristics, holding the worker's characteristics constant" (Brown, 1980). Despite its attempt to separate monetary and nonmonetary perception, the theory of equalizing differences could not go beyond the labor market due to its conceptual limitations.

The principles of behavioral economics addresses human ***bounded rationality*** and is based on human psychology applied to economic and business decisions (Kahneman and Tversky, 1979, 2000; Kahneman et al., 1982; Kahneman, 2011; Simon, 1955, 1972). Behavioral economics has implicitly addressed nonmonetary values by engaging subjective rules of thumb, beliefs, and hopes as major driving forces in economic decisions but still kept it closely tied up with the monetary values.

1.4 The Need for Distinction between Monetary and Nonmonetary Values

The fact, that human decisions on trades and actions are frequently based on factors beyond just money and include psychological factors and biases, is known for quite a long time. Barter economies constitute an important form of nonmonetary market interactions. The concept of utility introduced in neoclassical economics, the monetary asymmetry of decision function in behavioral economics as well as many other concepts and approaches have made multiple attempts to understand and describe the influence of psychological factors and biases in decision-making and market activities.

However, in all those former mentioned approaches, money and its perception on one hand, and nonmonetary factors such as needs, satisfaction, biases, perception of goods, services, and actions, and other psychological factors on the other hand, are typically combined together that does not allow for a detailed quantitative analysis of the influence of psychological factor on human decision making and market activities.

It is well known that the principal strategic goal of any for-profit company is to maximize their net present value. This leaves it unclear why companies spend money on charity, which reduces the companies' net present monetary value. The principal goal of not-for-profit organizations cannot be quantitatively formulated at all with money consideration only.

Analysis of competitive strategies and decision-making lacks the account for distinctive driving forces and quantitative approach for competitive power without distinct balance of monetary and nonmonetary components of value.

Individuals often make decisions by undermining or even ignoring monetary components of the perceived value. For example, an individual may reject a job with the higher salary in favor to the job that brings the better satisfaction. The balance of such a choice cannot be accurately estimated without a distinct consideration of the nonmonetary value of the job for such an individual.

This book introduces the concept of ***general value*** that includes both, monetary and nonmonetary components as separate parts of general perception of value which could be applied to any specific market or it segment as well as to the economy in general.

2 Introducing General Value

2.1 Monetary and Nonmonetary Components of Value

According to the classical and neoclassical views, goods and services are assigned certain values. In classical economics value is understood in terms of production cost (labor theory of value) while neoclassical economics defines value in terms of human perception of the level of satisfaction which is referred to as utility. Behavioral economics argues that humans make their decisions with limited rationality by using rules of thumb, hopes, and beliefs rather than with rational assessment of value. However, there is no contradiction between those views on value. Actually, humans do not need to calculate value accurately but use it only for comparison of goods or services when make decisions about exchange. An individual really needs to order the values of different goods or services to find out which one brings up a better satisfaction rather than accurately calculate the values. Such ordering is based on personal perception and is specific to each individual under given conditions. To do so, individuals may use their own subjective rules, beliefs and hopes, or quantify of the difference—rather than absolute quantity—of values of the compared goods or services.

Traditionally, the notion of value has been used in economics in its monetary meaning. However, there are nonmonetary values not directly related to money or its perception. Examples of such values are individual preference to certain activities, lifestyle, music, sciences, human relationships, and many others. Nonmonetary values contribute to human decisions along with monetary values. We define the term **general value** as a combination of monetary and nonmonetary values (Aityan, 2013). It can be assumed that the monetary and nonmonetary components are linearly related, i.e.

$$V_k = V_k^M + V_k^N \qquad (2.1)$$

where V_k is general value, V_k^M and V_k^N are monetary and nonmonetary components respectively, and index k identifies the individual because any judgment about value is subjective and specific to an individual. Both the monetary and nonmonetary components of value may in turn include different sub-components. For the sake of shortness, we will sometimes refer to general value simply as value.

2.2 Measuring General Value

To operate with the concept of general value it is necessary to know how to measure value and its components. The monetary component of value is traditionally measured either directly in units of money or in perception of money which is referred to as utility (Wicksteed, 1910; Stigler, 1950a, 1950b; Peterson & Lewis, 1998). Measuring monetary components of value in units of utility is more appropriate than doing it directly in the units of money because the utility approach reflects subjective perception of money by an individual. Different individuals or even the same individual under indifferent circumstances may have different perception of the same amount of money.

It is obvious that both components of value, monetary and nonmonetary, should be measured in the same units to enable comparison of both components because they are additive components of general value. Thus we could try to measure both components, monetary and nonmonetary, in the units similar the units of utility. The concept of utility for the monetary component is quite clear and has been used since the neoclassical period in economics. The nonmonetary component of value can be measured in parity with the monetary component of value. It is usually difficult to assess the nonmonetary values in terms comparable to the monetary values. "However, using the right tools, you can infer the worth of your comparative advantages and disadvantages" (Gale & Swire, 2006).

Measuring individual perception requires certain level of conceptual clarity and consistency. Economists of many generations have been engaged in pursuing this challenging task. Many different theories were introduced to measure subjective perception of values. There are two major concepts of utility: *cardinal utility* and *ordinal utility*. The concept of *cardinal utility* assumes that utility can be mapped to a numeric scale (Strotz, 1953) while the concept of *ordinal utility* (Pareto, 1906) addresses the case when the perception of a particular good or service cannot be measured using a numerical scale but can be only assessed in order of priority with alternative bundles (combinations) of goods—we can call it measuring in parity with alternatives. Another approach of dealing with consumer preferences was presented in the *revealed preference theory* (Samuelson, 1938) which assumes that consumers purchasing habits can reveal their preferences when consumers consider choices. Consumers may consider risky choices with different possible outcomes, decisions on which can be based on risk analysis. The model of *expected utility* was introduced to handle such situations (Bernoulli, 1738/1954; von Neumann & Morgenstern, 1944). Bernoulli derived his approach in the analysis of St. Petersburg lottery, often called the St. Petersburg paradox (Bernoulli, 1738). The St. Petersburg lottery is played by flipping a fair coin until it comes up tails, and the prize is equal to the total number of flips, n, which equals $\$2^n$ (Martin, 2011). The expected value of the game is an infinitely high. However "few of us would pay even \$25 to enter such a game" (Hacking, 1980).This paradox is based on the fact that most people do not follow a naïve decision criterion that takes only the expected value into account when possible reward is very high and possible loss is very low. Before the middle of twentieth century *expected utility* was called *moral expectation*. Regardless of the mathematical expected value people may make irrational decisions to avert or to seek risk. John von Neumann and Oscar Morgenstern (1944) applied the game theory to expected utility.

The Bernoulli approach laid foundations for the theory of *marginal utility* which is conventionally understood as an additional utility from an additional unit of a good or service. More accurately marginal utility is defined as a derivative of utility over the quantity of goods or services as

$$MU_k(Q) = \frac{dU_k(Q)}{dQ} \qquad (2.2)$$

where $MU_k(Q)$ is marginal utility for individual k, $U_k(Q)$ is the appropriate utility, and Q is quantity of the used entity (money, product, services).

Utility reflects individual perception of money, goods or services. Commonly accepted values in a society could be viewed as collective aggregate utility of all individuals in the society. An aggregate collective utility of a society can be represented by a *social welfare function* (Bergson, 1938, 1954; Samuelson, 1938). Different choices with the same perceived utility indicate the same level of satisfaction with the choices adopted by a given society.

Critics of marginal utility in *behavioral economics* (Simon, 1955; Kahneman et al., 1982; Kahneman et al, 2000; Kahneman, 2011) argues that this concept of marginal utility is applicable to rational actors while humans normally act irrationally and their behavior is mostly based on their psychology, rules of thumb, heuristics, and behavioral patterns rather than on accurate calculations. This criticism has merits and should be taken into consideration.

Regarding general value, we suggest measuring the nonmonetary components by indifference parity with the monetary component. It means that if an individual is equally willing to give up a certain quantity of monetary value for a certain increment of nonmonetary value or vice versa such a transaction or action does not change the total general value, i.e.

$$\Delta V_k = \Delta V_k^M + \Delta V_k^N = 0 \qquad (2.3)$$

where ΔV_k, ΔV_k^M, ΔV_k^N are marginal changes of general value and its monetary and nonmonetary components, respectively after and before the transaction or action. Thus, one can say that for any indifferent transaction or action the increment of the nonmonetary value is equal to the increment of the monetary value with the opposite sign, with the conservation of the general value, i.e.

$$\Delta V_k^M = -\Delta V_k^N \qquad (2.4)$$

We do not expect all humans to calculate the components of value accurately or rationally though it may be the case for some individuals. The components of general value could be assessed by an individual either rationally by calculating or irrationally with "bounded rationality" by applying rules of thumb, or any other human heuristics. Different individuals may make assessments differently depending on the personal choice of each individual.

The monetary and nonmonetary components of general value can be assessed in many different ways, rational or irrational. The major point of this approach is that individuals are somehow able to assess perceived differences of the components of general value, ΔV_k^M and ΔV_k^N, for the given choices in their own way. In conclusion, it should be mentioned that all components of general value are measured in units of individual perception which may be different for different individuals and even for the same individual in different circumstances.

2.3 Principle of Increasing General Value

Every transaction is an exchange of values between participants. However, there are some other activities outside the scope of transactions, i.e. activities, which are not associated with exchange, for example, the choice of an action. Any activity, either associated with an exchange or not, is referred to as action. Each participant makes a decision to pursue with an action if the resultant value (the general value after the action) for this participant is greater than the initial value (the general value before the action), i.e.

$$V_k^{after} \geq V_k^{before} \quad \text{or} \quad \Delta V_k = V_k^{after} - V_k^{before} > 0 \qquad (2.5)$$

for each participant k of the action. The difference between values after and before the action ΔV_k is referred to as the added value for the action undertaken by the participant. This statement can be paraphrased as: in result of any action, the added general value should gro.

Actions resulted in a positive added value are referred to as positive actions while actions resulted in a zero added value are referred to as neutral actions. Sometimes an action may result in a negative monetary value. However, it does not contradict the principle of increasing value because if an individual decides to pursue with the action despite a loss in the monetary value it means that the nonmonetary value of this action increases sufficiently enough to offset the loss of the monetary value in the added general value in this transaction to make the increment of the general value positive or at least zero. For example, any charity action leads to a monetary lose for the charity giver. However, the entire general value in that action increases due to a high nonmonetary component of the general value.

2.4 Special Cases and Examples

The following cases and examples are intended to illustrate and clarify the concept of general value.

2.4.1 Job Selection

If job A offers compensation S^A expressed in dollars, then the general value of this job for individual k is

$$V_k^A = U_k(S^A) + V_k^{NA} \qquad (2.6)$$

where $U_k(S^A)$ is the monetary value[2] of amount S^A and V_k^{NA} is the nonmonetary value of job A for individual k. The nonmonetary value of the job is measured in the same units as the monetary value for the individual, which could be interpreted in terms of parity with the monetary value. Suppose the same individual is offered another job B with compensation S^B and nonmonetary value V_k^{NB}, so the total (general) value of this job is

$$V_k^B = U_k(S^B) + V_k^{NB} \qquad (2.7)$$

---

[2] Monetary value can be measured either in terms of utility or in any other terms convenient for the individual, rationally or with bounded rationality. In some cases for the sake of simplicity we may consider neutral monetary value similar to neutral utility, i.e. $U(S) = S$, i.e. perception of money to be equal to the amount.

2 Introducing General Value

The individual will take a job which has the highest total value. The difference between values of job A and B for the individual is

$$\Delta V_k^{AB} = V_k^B - V_k^A = \left(U_k(S^B) - U_k(S^A)\right) + \left(V_k^{NB} - V_k^{NA}\right) = \\ = \Delta V_k^{MAB} + \Delta V_k^{NAB} \quad (2.8)$$

where $\Delta V_k^{MAB} = U_k(S^B) - U_k(S^A)$ is the difference of monetary values of jobs A and B and $\Delta V_k^{NAB} = V_k^{NB} - V_k^{NA}$ is the difference of nonmonetary values of these jobs for individual k. Note that, in general, $U_k(S^B) - U_k(S^A) \neq U_k(S^B - S^A)$. Suppose job B offers a lower compensation than job A, i.e. $\Delta V_k^{MAB} < 0$, but the nonmonetary value of job B is higher than the nonmonetary value of job A, i.e. $\Delta V_k^{NAB} > 0$ in such a way that total difference of general values of jobs A and B is in favor to job B, i.e. $\Delta V_k^{AB} > 0$. Then the individual will choose job B over job A. If for another individual the monetary value of job B is not as high compared to nonmonetary value of job A, then that individual will choose job A.

An Example

Suppose business graduate is offered a job of business analyst (job A) with annual compensation $60K. The same graduate is also offered another job of a garbage processing operator (job B) with the same annual compensation[3]. The graduate chooses job A because he likes it better. It means that

$$\Delta V_k^{AB} = \Delta V_k^{MAB} + \Delta V_k^{NAB} < 0 \quad (2.9)$$

where the difference between monetary values of these jobs equals zero, $\Delta V_k^{MAB} = 0$, because of equal compensations for both jobs while the difference of nonmonetary values of these jobs is in favor of job A for this individual, $\Delta V_k^{NAB} < 0$.

Suppose the compensation for job B is now increased to $200K. Most likely, the graduate will choose job B because the difference of the monetary values of jobs A and B is too high to

---

[3] For the sake of simplicity we do not consider other benefits offered by the employers

overtake the higher nonmonetary value of job *A* in comparison with job *B*, i.e.

$$\Delta V_k^{AB} = \Delta V_k^{MAB} + \Delta V_k^{NAB} > 0 \qquad (2.10)$$

Suppose the compensation for job *B* is $100K and in this situation, the graduate has no preference which job to choose. It occurs because the difference of the monetary values of jobs *A* and *B* is in favor of job *B* in the perception of the graduate, $\Delta V_k^{MAB} > 0$, while the nonmonetary value of job *B* is in favor of job *A*, $\Delta V_k^{NAB} < 0$, in such a way that

$$\Delta V_k^{AB} = \Delta V_k^{MAB} + \Delta V_k^{NAB} = 0 \qquad (2.11)$$

i.e. both jobs in the perception of the graduate have equal general values (Eq.(2.11)). In result, one can conclude that the difference in nonmonetary values of these two jobs compensate for the difference in the compensations in the perception of that particular person as

$$\Delta V_k^{NAB} = -\Delta V_k^{MAB} = -U_k(\$100K) + U_k(\$60K) \qquad (2.12)$$

because according to Eq. (2.11) the individual is indifferent (equally satisfied) about the jobs when compensation for job *A* is $60K and for job *B* is $100K.

Let's assume this particular individual has a neutral perception of money, i.e. $U_k(S) = S$ at the time of choice, so the difference between nonmonetary values of job *A* and *B* is

$$\begin{aligned}\Delta V_k^{NAB} &= -U_k(\$100K) + U_k(\$60K) = \\ &= -\$100K + \$60K = -\$40K\end{aligned} \qquad (2.13)$$

where $U_k(\$100K) = \$100K$ and $U_k(\$60K) = \$60K$. It means that in case of the indifferent choice, the difference of nonmonetary values of jobs *A* and *B*, ΔV_k^{NAB}, is equal to the difference of compensations for the jobs with the opposite sign, $-\Delta V_k^{MAB}$.

2.4.2 Transaction Decisions

Individual k comes to a bakery to buy a loaf of bread at price P. Before the act of exchange (purchase), the individual has the money and the baker (denote him with index n) has the bread. Thus, the individual and the baker have the following values before the transaction

$$V_k^{before} = U_k(P) \quad \text{and} \quad V_n^{before} = V_n^{Bread} \qquad (2.14)$$

and after the transaction their values are

$$V_k^{after} = V_k^{Bread} \quad \text{and} \quad V_n^{after} = U_n(P) \qquad (2.15)$$

The added values in this transaction for the individual and the baker are

$$\begin{aligned} \Delta V_k &= -U_k(P) + V_k^{Bread} > 0; \\ \Delta V_n &= U_n(P) - V_n^{Bread} > 0 \end{aligned} \qquad (2.16)$$

Both parties, the individual and the baker, agree on the transaction if the added values for both are positive. It means that value of having the loaf of bread for the individual is higher than the value of amount of money P while for the baker the value of amount P is higher than the value of the bread. Neither the individual nor the baker agree to do the transaction if in result they lose general value.

2.4.3 A Buying Choice

Suppose individual k considers buying a pair of shoes for his personal use. There are two different pairs of shoes A and B at prices P^A and P^B, respectively, available in the store. If the individual buys shoes A or B his added value will be

$$\Delta V_k^A = -U_k(P^A) + V_k^{NA} \quad \text{or} \quad \Delta V_k^B = -U_k(P^B) + V_k^{NB} \qquad (2.17)$$

The monetary part in the added value comes from the price paid by the individual for the shoes. It is included in the added value with the negative sign because it is part of the value the individual had before the transaction, i.e. the money which the individual paid for the shoes. On the other hand, V_k^{NA} and V_k^{NB} are the nonmonetary values for the individual of having shoes A and B, respectively. These components of value are added with the positive sign because it is the acquired value after transaction as shown below.

$$V_k^{A\,before} = -U_k(P^A) \quad \text{and} \quad V_k^{B\,before} = -U_k(P^B) \\ V_k^{A\,after} = V_k^{NA} \qquad\qquad V_k^{B\,after} = V_k^{NB}$$ (2.18)

The individual makes a buying decision based on the added value rather than on the price only. For simplicity, we consider neutral monetary utility, i.e. $U_k(P) = P$ for individual k. Suppose shoes A are more expensive than shoes B, i.e. $P^A > P^B$, but both prices are within the individual's budget for shoes. On the other hand, if the individual likes shoes A better than shoes B, that the difference of the nonmonetary values of this shows for individual k is greater than the inverse difference of the monetary values, so the added value of shows A as higher than the added value of shoes B, i.e. $\Delta V_k^A > \Delta V_k^B$ then the individual buys shoes A.

If the same individual has limitations of money he can spend on shoes, then a certain difference in prices $P^B - P^A$ may project to a greater difference in monetary components of value $U_k(P^B) - U_k(P^A)$, which, in turn, may lead to $\Delta V_k^A < \Delta V_k^B$ then individual k makes a decision to buy shows B.

2.4.4 Trading Decisions

Suppose party k trades with party n. Party k trades (exchanges) product A for product B of party n. Both products have different monetary and nonmonetary values for each party. Products A and B could be, for instance, collectible ancient golden and silver coins which have monetary (market) values, and nonmonetary (personal collectible) values. The monetary value of the coin goes beyond just commodity value of it but is defined by the market value of the coin which includes its overall collectible value. Personal collectible value may come, for instance, from the fact that the collection of individual k is missing coin B that creates some additional value of the coin for individual k. Let's for simplicity presume that both traders, k and n have neutral utility for money, i.e. $U_k(P) = U_n(P) = P$. Before the trade the parties have the following values

$$V_k^{before} = P^A + V_k^{NA} \quad \text{and} \quad V_n^{before} = P^B + V_n^{NB}$$ (2.19)

2 Introducing General Value

After the trade, the values possessed by these parties will be

$$V_k^{after} = P^B + V_k^{NB} \quad \text{and} \quad V_n^{after} = P^A + V_n^{NA} \quad (2.20)$$

where V_k^{NA}, V_k^{NB}, V_n^{NA}, and V_n^{NB} are the nonmonetary values of coins A and B for parties k and n. Parties k and n will be willing to do the trade if the general value possessed by parties k and n after the trade are greater than the values before the trade, i.e.

$$\begin{aligned}\Delta V_k = V_k^{after} - V_k^{before} = V_k^{NB} - V_k^{NA} + \Delta P^{AB} > 0 \\ \Delta V_n = V_n^{after} - V_n^{before} = V_n^{NA} - V_n^{NB} - \Delta P^{AB} > 0\end{aligned} \quad (2.21)$$

where $\Delta P^{AB} = P^B - P^A$ represents the difference in monetary values between coins A and B. Thus, party k and party n are willing to pursue with the trade if both parties increase or at least keep unchanged their values, i.e.

$$\begin{aligned}V_k^{NB} - V_k^{NA} > -\Delta P^{AB} \\ V_n^{NA} - V_n^{NB} > \Delta P^{AB}\end{aligned} \quad (2.22)$$

If both coins have the same monetary (market) values, i.e. $P^A = P^B$ or $\Delta P^{AB} = 0$, then the transaction will take place if party k likes coin B better than coin A and party n likes coin B better than coin A. It may occur, for instance, if party k misses coin B in his collection and party n misses coin A in his collection or for many other reasons unrelated to the market value of the coins.

2.4.5 My Kingdom for a Horse

In Richard III, a history play by Shakespeare, King Richard III being unhorsed in a climax of a battle cried out, "*A horse, a horse, my kingdom for a horse!*" Let's analyze this phrase from the point of view of general value.

The general value of a horse in the perception of the king, V_k^H, is

$$V_k^H = U_k(P^H) + V_k^{NH} \quad (2.23)$$

where P^H is the market price of the horse, $U_k(P^H)$, is the utility of the price for the horse in a perception of the king, and V_k^{NH} is the nonmonetary value of this horse for the king. The general value of the kingdom for the king is V_k^K which is very high but limited. We will not even divide it into monetary and nonmonetary components because it is not necessary for the purpose of this example.

The general value of the horse V_k^H and the general value of his kingdom V_k^K for Richard III in a normal situation are related as $V_k^H \ll V_k^K$ and for this reason, the king does not even consider trading his kingdom for a horse. However, when his life became threatened in the battle, the perceived nonmonetary value of a horse $\overline{V_k^H}$ significantly exceeded the value of his kingdom, $\overline{V_k^H} > V_k^K$, and for this reason trading the kingdom for a horse became a viable idea for him.

2.4.6 Gresham's Law

The well-known Gresham's law reads that *"bad money drives good money out of circulation"*[4]. Let's analyze this law from the point of view of general value. Suppose there are two types of money, money A and B, and all people have similar perception of both components of value. The general value V^α of money α (α = A,B) is

$$V^\alpha = V^{\alpha,Nom} + V^{\alpha,Comm} + V^{N\alpha} \qquad (2.24)$$

where $V^{\alpha,Nom}$ is the nominal value, $V^{\alpha,Comm}$ is the additional commodity value, and $V^{N\alpha}$ is the nonmonetary value of money α. Both nominal and commodity values belong to the monetary component of value. The nonmonetary value of money may come from its condition (a crispy bill or a shiny coin), antiquity (coin age), or collectability (rareness and show quality) or any other features.

---

[4] Some sources argue about this statement however such a discussion is irrelevant to the purpose of the present example <http://eh.net/encyclopedia/article/selgin.gresham.law>.

2 Introducing General Value

Fiat Money versus Commodity Money

Suppose money A is paper (fiat) money and money B is gold (commodity) money. Both paper and commodity money have the same nominal value, different commodity values, and the same (maybe zero) nonmonetary value. i.e.

$$V^{A,Nom} = V^{B,Nom}; \quad V^{A,Comm} < V^{B,Comm}; \quad V^{NA} = V^{NB} \qquad (2.25)$$

and thus

$$V^A < V^B \qquad (2.26)$$

The assumption of equal nonmonetary values of both kinds of money in this example is taken only for the purpose of simplicity.

According to the differences in general values of paper and gold money, we definitely prefer to use paper money and keep gold money, i.e. to use the money with the lower general value and keep the money with the higher general value. It proves the Gresham's law from the perspective of general value.

Crisp Bills versus Worn Bills

You may recall a situation when paying in stores you prefer to pay with worn bills and keep new crispy bills of the same nominal value. Both crisp, A, and worn, B, bills have the same nominal value, equal and actually zero commodity values, and different nonmonetary values because we just prefer crispy bills in our valet. It means

$$V_k^{A,Nom} = V_k^{B,Nom}; \quad V_k^{A,Comm} = V_k^{B,Comm}; \quad V_k^{NA} > V_k^{NB} \qquad (2.27)$$

where $V_k^{X,Nom}$, $V_k^{X,Comm}$, V_k^{NX} are the nominal, commodity, and nonmonetary values of bill X, correspondently. The nominal and commodity values constitute the monetary component of the general value. The difference between nonmonetary values of crisp and worn bills can be explained by a simple fact that we like crisp bills better than worn bills. It makes the general value of crisp bills higher than the general value of the worn ones,

$$V^A > V^B \qquad (2.28)$$

Thus, according to the difference in general values, we keep crisp bills and pay with worn ones.

2.5 Isovalue

If all job offers considered in the example in section 2.4.1 above have equal general values $V_k^A = V_k^B = ... = V_k^Z$ while their monetary (offered compensations) and nonmonetary components are different, then individual k will be indifferent (equally satisfied) in choosing any job from the given jobs. The jobs which offer the same general value constitute an *isovalue* line in the space of monetary and nonmonetary values. In case of linear relationship between monetary and nonmonetary components of the general value as in Eq. (2.1), *isovalues* form a set of parallel lines, one for each level of general value as shown in Figure 2-1.

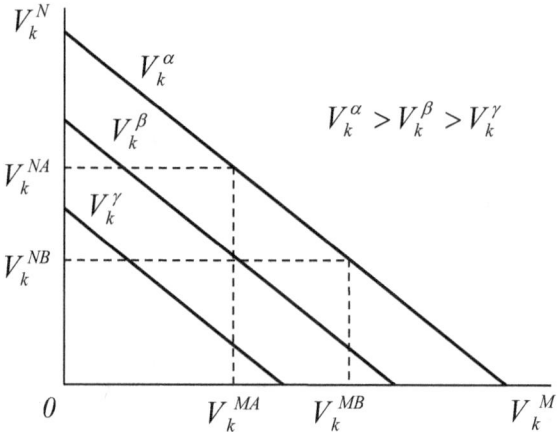

Figure 2-1: Isovalues in the monetary-nonmonetary space

For instance, if an individual equally considers two jobs, one with monetary value (annual compensation) $V_k^{MA} = U_k(S^A) = U_k(\$60K)$ and another with $V_k^{MB} = U_k(S^B) = U_k(\$100K)$, it means that the difference of monetary values of jobs A and B, $\Delta V_k^{MAB} = V_k^{MB} - V_k^{MA}$, is compensated by the difference of nonmonetary values of these jobs, $\Delta V_k^{NAB} = V_k^{NB} - V_k^{NA}$, as $\Delta V_k^{NAB} = -\Delta V_k^{MAB}$. It means that we may be equally satisfied with different jobs even if one of them pays less than another just because we like the first

2 Introducing General Value

job better. Most likely, most of us have faced a similar dilemma in our lives.

2.6 Business Analysis

The concept of general value can be applied in business analysis.

2.6.1 The General Goal of a Business

Traditional View

The general goal of a for-profit business is typically defined as maximization of the owners' wealth which translates into maximization of the net present value of the business, where value is traditionally understood in its monetary meaning. This is a quite crisp and measurable definition. However, when we talk about a not-for-profit organization, the definition of the general goal of such an organization becomes quite vague, fuzzy, and non-measurable. Moreover, if we talk about a for-profit company, the traditional definition of the general goal gets in conflict with social and charitable activities of the company. It leads to a conclusion that as soon as any social and charitable activity results in a monetary loss, such an activity should be avoided. It is clear that such an approach suffers serious deficiency.

View from General Value

Let's consider general value of a business as a combination of the monetary and the monetary components, as

$$V_k = V_k^M + V_k^N \qquad (2.29)$$

where index k identifies the perception of the company owners or management team. The general goal of the company is defined as maximization of the net present general value of it. This definition fits all, for-profit companies, not-for-profit organization, and any combination of them. In an extreme case of a "completely greedy" for-profit company the nonmonetary component of the general value equals zero and the company should be concerned only about monetary value as in a traditional approach. In an extreme case of a pure not-for-profit organization the monetary component of the general value equals zero and the organization should maximize its net-present general value by maximizing only net present nonmonetary part of it. For a real-world for-profit company maximization of net present general value includes both components. It means that the company may give up some monetary gains for nonmonetary gains to maximize the net total general value. Most for-profit companies are engaged in free-of-charge social services and charities. The tradeoff between monetary and nonmonetary components depends on the company's perception of value. For example, if a company believes that additional benefits for its employee or a charitable activity, which do not directly translate into company monetary value, add more to the company general value than an additional monetary gain given up for such benefits or charitable activities, the general value of the company grows and the company goes for it in accordance to its general goal and the company's perception of values. A similar consideration could be given to any company or organization regardless of whether it is a for-profit company or a not-for-profit organization.

2.6.2 Opportunity Decisions

Suppose individual k has to make a decision either to go to a theater or to do some work for money. If the individual goes to the theater, he has to pay \$100 for a ticket but if the individual decides to spend that time working, he will make \$150. What does drive the individual's decision?

The general value of going to the theater is

$$V_k^T = -P^T + V_k^{NT} \tag{2.30}$$

where P^T is the price of a theater ticket (monetary value) and V_k^{NT} is the nonmonetary value of enjoying a play in the theater for individual k. On the other hand, the value of going to work is

$$V_k^W = P^W + V_k^{NW} \tag{2.31}$$

where P^W is the compensation (monetary value) which the individual gets for that period at work and V_k^{NW} is the nonmonetary value for individual k of going to work including a possible necessity to it. This nonmonetary value could be positive or negative, subject to how much the individual enjoys or hate the work and the necessity to do it. The difference of general values of going to the theater and going to work is

2 Introducing General Value

$$\Delta V_k^{TW} = V_k^W - V_k^T = P^W + P^T + V_k^{NW} - V_k^{NT} \qquad (2.32)$$

Thus if $\Delta V_k^{TW} > 0$, then the individual decides to go to work but if $\Delta V_k^{TW} < 0$ then the individual chooses to go to the theater. If $\Delta V_k^{TW} = 0$ then the individual is indifferent about the choice of action. Monetary values in Eqs. (2.30) – (2.32) for the sake of simplicity were expressed in nominal money rather than in perception of money.

For example, many teachers are giving extra classes to their students without additional compensation, just because they see a high nonmonetary value of this activity. Very often, teachers give up their entertainment and come to school to give their students extra classes. If a teacher does not see a sufficient nonmonetary value of this action, this teacher would not do it.

2.7 Difference between General Value and Utility

The concept of general value and the neoclassical concept of utility both address human perception of value. Critics of the suggested approach may argue that the concept of general value is identical to the concept of utility. Actually, both concepts address humans' individual perception. However, there is a fundamental difference between these two concepts.

The concept of utility represents satisfaction from the usage, possession, or exchange of money, goods, or services. Both, satisfaction from money as well as satisfaction from the nonmonetary aspects of goods, services, and other entities are inseparably combined in the concept of neoclassical utility. Such an approach can easily lead to confusion between the internal nonmonetary satisfaction related to the human perception of a good, a service, or any other entity and its exchangeability in the market related to the monetary aspects. The confusion with neoclassical utility may grow further in an attempt to understand the impact of monetary and nonmonetary factors on a decision and the relationship between these factors.

The concept of general value specifically and distinctly differentiates the perception of perceived nonmonetary satisfaction with goods, services, or other entities from the satisfaction with the amount of money associated with the goods, services, or other entities. Such a separation provides a solid and unambiguous ground for the assessment of value. The explicit distinction between monetary and nonmonetary components of value provides a clear separation of the monetary perception related to a transaction or exchange from the nonmonetary perception of value which might be unrelated to any transaction or any exchange. The nonmonetary component of value reflects a purely subjective perception of value independent of its monetary part. Thus, the concept of general value provides a more explicit and a less speculative approach for the assessment of subjective perception in a broad variety of entities in economics.

The concept of utility is synonymous to the concept of value in neoclassical economics. On the other hand, the concept of general value separates monetary and nonmonetary components of value and may use the neoclassical utility of money to express the perception of the monetary component of general value. Such a separation explains the difference between price, perception of money, and value.

Finally, the concept of general value is a good match for the explanation of perceived value in terms of behavioral economics.

2.8 Summarizing the Concept of General Value

This chapter introduced the concept of general value that consists of two components—monetary and nonmonetary. The nonmonetary component of value reflects individual perception unrelated to the perception of monetary part of value. Both components of value can be measured in units of human perception either rationally similar to the units of utility or with "bounded rationality" as suggested in behavioral economics, or in any other units which are appropriate and convenient to use. The fundamental difference between the concept of general value and conventional concept of value is in a separation of values unrelated to money from the values related to money. Both monetary and nonmonetary components of general value represent two sides of the perception of value.

To operate with the notion of general value one has to be able to compare monetary and non-monetary components for a single actor (an individual or a group of individuals) and compare values of different actors rather than accurately measure them. To make a decision an individual needs to assess a difference or to order values rather than to accurately calculate the values themselves. Actors are not expected to be completely rational as assumed in neoclassical economics and may act with "bounded rationality" as assumed in behavioral economics

Every action or transaction decision obeys the principle of increasing the general value of every participant. General value, is believed, constitutes a more comprehensive foundation of economics than traditionally accepted pure monetary value.

General value in economics plays a similar role as energy in physics. This analogy may be extended to the principles of equilibrium. It would be reasonable to assume that each transaction or action tends to bring an economic system to a state with the highest added value similarly to a trend of physical system to get to a state with the lowest energy in equilibrium. Thus, we can refer to general value as "***economic energy***."

The concept of general value goes beyond the classical and neoclassical views on value. The approach of general value helps make judgments and make decisions in a much broader scale of situations than just in market exchange.

The concept of general value provides a solid foundation for analysis of fundamental processes and decisions in economics for which the neoclassical concept of utility falls short of conceptual integrity and clarity (Aityan, 2013, 2020a, 2020b, Aityan et al., 2016, 2017).

3 Measuring the Nonmonetary Component of Value

3.1 Units for Measuring Nonmonetary Value

Both monetary and nonmonetary components of general value should be measured in the same units because they are additive to each other according to Eq.(2.1) from the previous chapter. The monetary component of general value can be measured in terms of perception of the amount of money. Such perception could be expressed in terms of utility of money as in neoclassical economics or in terms of value function as in behavioral economics. In case of the neutral perception of money, monetary value can be measured as nominal amount of money. Nonmonetary value should be measured in the same units as the monetary value though the nonmonetary value is not money at all.

In the range of amount of money, where the utility (perception) of money for the given individual is linearly depends on the amount, the monetary value may be measured in terms of the amount and thus, the nonmonetary value as well. Such an approximation would not affect the outcome but only makes the assessment easier. However, if the perception of money nonlinearly depends on the amount, both monetary and nonmonetary components should be measure in terms of utility of money.

3.2 The Indifference Point

When comparing two choices or two scenarios. the difference of nonmonetary values (a relative nonmonetary value) can be conveniently measured at the point of indifference, i.e. in the condition, when the difference of general values of two scenarios is equal to zero. The point of indifference means that a given individual does not have any preference in choosing between two scenarios, A and B. It means that general values of both choices, A and B, are equal to the individual, i.e.

$$V_A^M + V_A^N = V_B^M + V_B^N \qquad (3.1)$$

where V_A^M and V_A^N are the monetary and nonmonetary components of general value for scenario A and V_B^M and V_B^N are monetary and nonmonetary components of general value, respectively, for scenario B in the perception of the individual.

The nonmonetary component of value represents the internal perception of the individual while the monetary component of value is the external exchange value represented by the amount of money or its perception. For this reason, the indifference point can be reached by varying the monetary value – actually or virtually - to the point, when the individual becomes indifferent between the choices. At such a point the difference of the monetary values of two given choices gets compensated by the inverse difference of the nonmonetary values of those choices, equalizing general values of two choices.

The simplest way of finding the indifference point for two choices is to set up the monetary value of one of the choices, then vary the monetary value of another choice until the individual becomes indifferent in his/her choice. The indifference between choices means that the general value of these choice are equal (Eq. (3.1))

3 Measuring the Nonmonetary Component of Value

According to Eq.(3.1), the difference of general values of the choices or scenarios at the point of indifference equals zero, i.e.

$$\Delta V_{AB} = \Delta V_{AB}^M + \Delta V_{AB}^N = 0 \qquad (3.2)$$

where ΔV_{AB}^M and ΔV_{AB}^N are the relative monetary and nonmonetary values (differences of monetary and nonmonetary components of general values) for two scenarios A and B, i.e.

$$\Delta V_{AB}^M = \Delta V_A^M - \Delta V_B^M \quad \text{and} \quad \Delta V_{AB}^N = \Delta V_A^N - \Delta V_B^N \qquad (3.3)$$

We will refer to the difference of monetary and nonmonetary values as the relative monetary and nonmonetary value, respectively. Then the relative nonmonetary value of scenarios A and B can be calculated as a relative monetary value with the opposite sign as

$$\Delta V_{AB}^N = -\Delta V_{AB}^M \qquad (3.4)$$

Eq.(3.4) implies that the individual is indifferent in the choice of gaining an increment of the nonmonetary value for giving up the same increment of monetary value or vice versa.

Nonmonetary value also could vary in the individual perception. This could be impacted by advertisement, explanation or by cultural, family, religious, and social factors. In nowadays, media and the internet play a crucial role in setting up standards for nonmonetary values.

3.3 General Value of Jobs

3.3.1 General Value in Assessment of Jobs

Suppose an individual is choosing between two jobs, A and B, with the monetary compensations, S_A and S_B, correspondently. The general values of the jobs in the perception of the individual can be presented as

$$\begin{aligned} V_A &= V_A^M + V_A^N = U(S_A) + V_A^N \\ V_B &= V_B^M + V_B^N = U(S_B) + V_B^N \end{aligned} \qquad (3.5)$$

where $U(S_A)$ and $U(S_A)$ are the monetary values of the jobs, which reflect the monetary compensations in the terms of perception of money, V_A^N and V_B^N are the nonmonetary values of the jobs in the perception of the individual. Both components are taken with the positive sign because they both adding up the value of the job. The nonmonetary value of a job reflects the individual preferences related to the interest in the job, job prestige, working environment, commuting convenience, and many other nonmonetary factors. The monetary value in Eq.(3.5) is represented with the utility of money rather than with the amount of money due to a possibility of non-neutral (nonlinear) perception of different amounts of money by the individual and/or of the perception of the same amount of compensation by different individuals, or by the same individual due to different circumstances. The perception of the same amount could vary if, for example, the individual desperately needs money or the offered compensation does not cover the individual's required budget, or for many other reasons.

For the sake of generality, please note that in case of buying a good or a service, the monetary value, which reflects the perception of the price paid for a good or service, is included in general value with the negative sign because the price paid for the good or service reduces its general value; the higher price the lower is the general value.

3.3.2 Choice of a Job

When comparing jobs A and B, the difference of general values of these two jobs can be expressed as the difference of the monetary and nonmonetary values of these jobs for a given individual as

$$\Delta V_{AB} = V_A - V_B = \Delta V_{AB}^M + \Delta V_{AB}^N \qquad (3.6)$$

where

$$\begin{aligned} \Delta V_{AB}^M &= V_A^M - V_B^M = U(S_A) - U(S_B) \\ \Delta V_{AB}^N &= V_A^N - V_B^N \end{aligned} \qquad (3.7)$$

An individual chooses a job that offers a higher general value rather than a higher monetary compensation alone as shown in Eq.(3.8):

3 Measuring the Nonmonetary Component of Value

$$\Delta V_{AB} > 0 \rightarrow \Delta V_{AB}^N > -(U(S_A) - U(S_B)) \rightarrow \text{Preference of job } A$$
$$\Delta V_{AB} < 0 \rightarrow \Delta V_{AB}^N < -(U(S_A) - U(S_B)) \rightarrow \text{Preference of job } B \quad (3.8)$$
$$\Delta V_{AB} = 0 \rightarrow \Delta V_{AB}^N = -(U(S_A) - U(S_B)) \rightarrow \text{No preference}$$

Figure 3-1 shows an example when an individual chooses job A over job B despite the lower monetary compensation offered for job A. The choice is caused by the higher general value due the higher nonmonetary value of job B for the individual

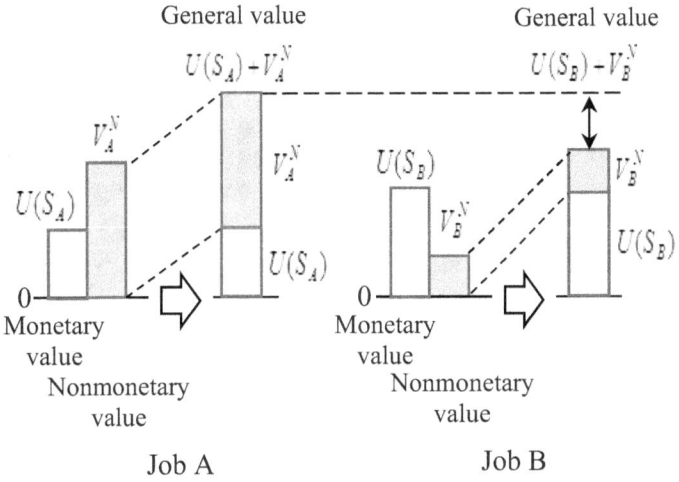

Figure 3-1: An example of choosing jobs A over job B, by an individual despite a lower compensation offered for job A due to a higher nonmonetary value of job A

As is evident from Figure 3-1, the individual chooses job A over job B because the general value of job A is higher than the general value of job B for this particular individual. The choice was made in favor of job A despite the lower monetary compensation for job A than for job B.

3.3.3 Assessment of the Same Job by Different Individuals

Different people may differently assess general value of the same job. Suppose two individuals, k and m, are offered the same job with the same monetary compensation, S, and the same work conditions. Assume that both job candidates are neutral in their perception of money, so

$$U_k(S) = U_m(S) = S \qquad (3.9)$$

where $U_k(S)$ and $U_m(S)$ are utilities of money for individuals k and m.

Both candidates are equally qualified for the job. However the job responsibilities imply working in shifts. Job candidate k likes working in shifts because he studies at university while candidate m prefers working regular hours because he is married with children. For this reason, the nonmonetary value of the job is different for these job candidates, i.e.

$$V_k^N > V_m^N \qquad (3.10)$$

Due to different nonmonetary values and equal monetary values of the job for these individuals, the general value of the job for candidate k is greater than one for candidate m, i.e.

$$V_k > V_m \qquad (3.11)$$

In result, candidate k will be more incline to accept the job offer than candidate m as shown in Figure 3-2.

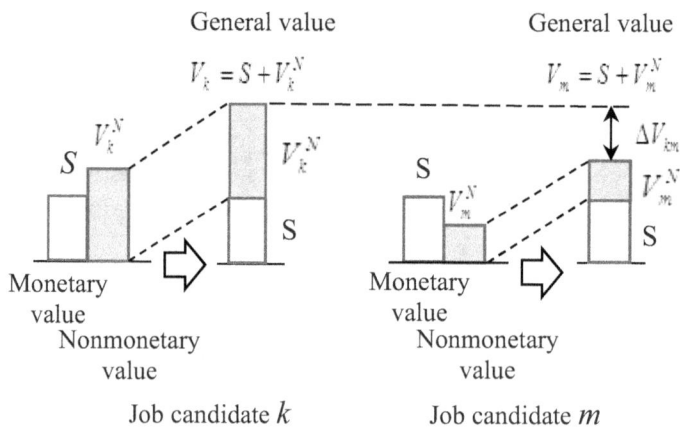

Figure 3-2: An example of the same job assessment by two different individuals, k and m

The difference of general values of the job between job candidates k and m, shown in Figure 3-2, is

3 Measuring the Nonmonetary Component of Value

$$\Delta V_{km} = V_k - V_m = V_k^M + V_k^N - V_m^M - V_m^N = $$
$$= \Delta V_k^M - \Delta V_k^N = -\Delta V_{km}^N \qquad (3.12)$$

where

$$\Delta V_{km}^M = V_k^M - V_m^M = S - S = 0$$
$$\Delta V_{km}^N = V_k^N - V_m^N \qquad (3.13)$$

Let's note that in case of a job, the monetary component is included in general value with the positive sign as shown in Eq.(3.5) because the higher monetary compensation, the higher general value of the job. On the other hand, as was discussed above, the monetary component (the perception of price) is included in general value of a good or a service for consumers with the negative sign, because the higher price, the less general value the appropriate good or service has in the perception of the consumer.

3.3.4 Measuring the Difference of Nonmonetary Values of Jobs

The difference of the general values of two jobs A and B, in the perception of an individual, equals zero at the indifference point as expressed in Eq.(3.2), hence the difference of the nonmonetary values of jobs A and B in the perception of that individual can be measured according to Eqs.(3.4) and (3.7) as the difference of the monetary values of these jobs with the negative sign, i.e.

$$\Delta V_{AB}^N = -(U(S_A) - U(S_B)) \qquad (3.14)$$

where S_A and S_B are the monetary compensations for jobs A and B, accordingly. The utility of the monetary compensation $U(S)$ reflects the perception of amount S by the given individual. Such perception may depend on many factors such as general circumstances, lack of savings, certain commitments or obligations, and many other factors.

Let's use for simplicity the neutral utility, i.e. neutral perception of money where the perception of money just matches the amount as

$$U(S) = S \qquad (3.15)$$

where S is the amount of money and $U(S)$ is its perception by the individual.

With the neutral perception of money, the difference of nonmonetary values of jobs can be measured simply as a difference of monetary compensations with the opposite sign, i.e.

$$\Delta V^N_{AB} = -(S_A - S_B) = -\Delta S_{AB} \qquad (3.16)$$

where ΔS_{AB} is the difference of the monetary values of jobs A and B. It is evident that the relative general value (the difference of the general values) of any two jobs, including its components, relative monetary and nonmonetary values, obeys the anticommutativity rule, i.e. relative general value of A and B, including its relative monetary and nonmonetary components, is equal to the relative nonmonetary value of B and A with the opposite sign as shown below

$$\Delta V^N_{BA} = -\Delta V^N_{AB} \quad \text{and} \quad \Delta S_{BA} = -\Delta S_{AB} \qquad (3.17)$$

The major point of the methodology is that the difference of the nonmonetary values (relative nonmonetary value) of any two jobs for a given individual can be measured by the difference of the monetary values (relative monetary value) of these jobs at the indifference point for this individual. It is expected that specific social groups may share similar nonmonetary values of jobs. These common nonmonetary values within a social group can be found from a survey conducted in the group.

3.4 General Value in Purchasing Decision

3.4.1 Choice of a Consumption Product

By term ***product*** we understand goods or services, i.e. everything that is available for purchase.

Suppose an individual has to make a decision on buying either product A or product B with the respective prices P_A and P_B. The general value resulted from buying product A would be V_A and the general value resulted from buying product B would be V_B

$$\begin{aligned} V_A &= V^M_A + V^N_A = -U(P_A) + V^N_A \\ V_B &= V^M_B + V^N_B = -U(P_B) + V^N_B \end{aligned} \qquad (3.18)$$

3 Measuring the Nonmonetary Component of Value 41

where $U(P_A)$ and $U(P_B)$ are the monetary components of purchasing products A and B expressed in the terms of perception of the respective amount of money. The monetary value in Eq.(3.18) is presented with the negative sign because the price is paid by the individual, i.e. the higher price the lower is the monetary value of the product for the individual. This applies to the consumption products which are no intended for a resale.

The nonmonetary values of the products are positive if the buyer expects satisfaction with the products. The individual may expect different level of satisfaction with different products that results in different nonmonetary values of the products. An example of general values of products A and B according to Eq. (3.1) is shown in Figure 3-3. The general value of product A, as the sum of monetary and nonmonetary values, is positive for the buyer in the example presented in Figure 3-3, i.e. the nonmonetary value is higher than the monetary value (the price), that leads to a favorable decision about buying the product. The nonmonetary value of product B is lower than the negative monetary value of the product, thus the general value of product B is negative for the buyer. This leads to the unfavorable decision about buying the product. In result, the individual considers buying product A but rejects buying product B.

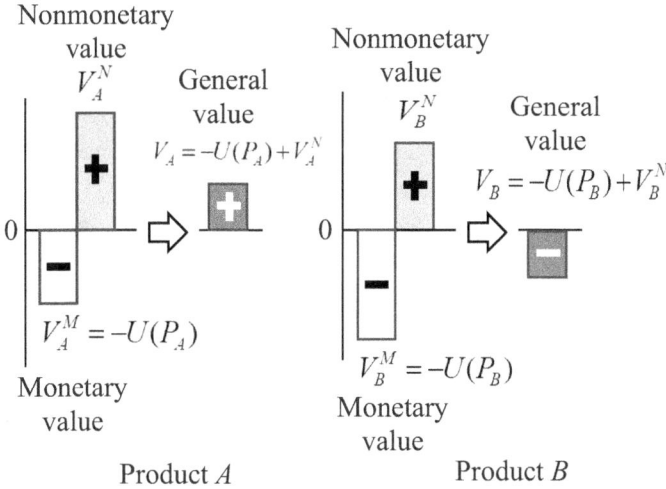

Figure 3-3: An example of the added general value of purchasing product A or B according to Eq.(3.18)

Let's note that in case of buying goods or using services, price contributes to general value of a good or a service with the negative sign because the higher price the lower the value the appropriate good or service for the buyer. On the other hand, the job compensation in case of jobs contributes to the general value with the positive sign because the higher compensation the higher general value of the job (Aityan et al., 2016).

3.4.2 Comparison of Products

In a comparative assessment of two products, say, product A and product B, the individual compares their general values as

$$\Delta V_{AB} = V_A - V_B = \Delta V_{AB}^M - \Delta V_{AB}^N \qquad (3.19)$$

where ΔV_{AB}^M and ΔV_{AB}^N are the differences of monetary and nonmonetary values of products A and B, i.e.

$$\begin{aligned}\Delta V_{AB}^M &= V_A^M - V_B^M = -(U(P_A) - U(P_B)) \\ \Delta V_{AB}^N &= V_A^N - V_B^N\end{aligned} \qquad (3.20)$$

If the individual shows neutral perception of money, i.e.

$$U(P) = P \qquad (3.21)$$

then Eq.(3.18) for general values can be rewritten in terms of amount rather than in terms of utility of money, i.e.

$$V_A = -P_A + V_A^N \quad \text{or} \quad V_B = -P_B + V_B^N \qquad (3.22)$$

thus

$$\begin{aligned}\Delta V_{AB}^M &= V_A^M - V_B^M = -(U(P_A) - U(P_B)) = -(P_A - P_B) \\ \Delta V_{AB}^N &= V_A^N - V_B^N\end{aligned} \qquad (3.23)$$

The difference of general values of products A and B, ΔV_{AB}, defines the individual's preference between the products. If $\Delta V_{AB} > 0$ then the individual prefers product A, if $\Delta V_{AB} < 0$ the individual prefers product B, and if $\Delta V_{AB} = 0$ the individual is indifferent about the products. These choices are presented in Eq.(3.24) below.

3 Measuring the Nonmonetary Component of Value

$$
\begin{array}{llll}
\text{if } \Delta V_{AB}^N > \Delta P_{AB} & \to & \Delta V_{AB} > 0 & \to \text{ Preference of product } A \\
\text{if } \Delta V_{AB}^N < \Delta P_{AB} & \to & \Delta V_{AB} < 0 & \to \text{ Preference of product } B \\
\text{if } \Delta V_{AB}^N = \Delta P_{AB} & \to & \Delta V_{AB} = 0 & \to \text{ No preference}
\end{array}
\quad (3.24)
$$

where

$$\Delta P_{AB} = P_A - P_B \qquad (3.25)$$

As is evident from Eq.(3.24), the preference of one product over another is determined by the relationship between the differences in the monetary and the nonmonetary values of the products. Product A may be more expensive than product B but shows a sufficiently higher nonmonetary value to be chosen over product B.

An example of a comparison of products A and B is shown in Figure 3-4. Both products show positive general values in the perception of individual k but product A has a higher general value than product B, i.e. $\Delta V_{AB} > 0$, that results in the preference of product A over product B.

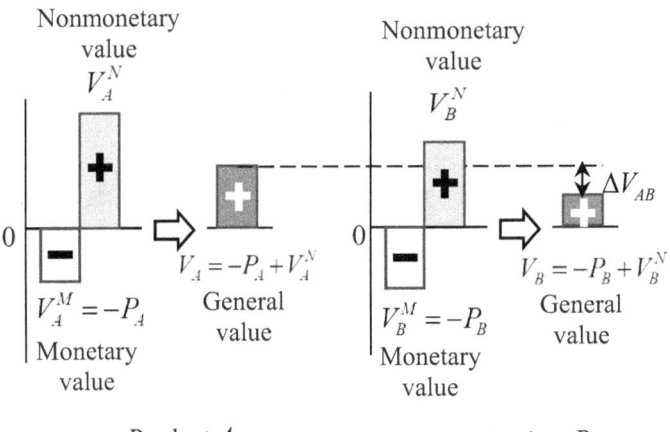

Figure 3-4: An example of the choice between two products, A or B, for an individual with neutral perception of money, i.e. with $U(P) = P$ and according to Eq.(3.24)

The difference of the nonmonetary components of value of products A and B, ΔV_{AB}^N, at the indifference point can be found from Eq.(3.24) from the difference of their monetary components. In the assumption of neutral perception of the amount of money by the individual the difference of the nonmonetary components of value is

$$\Delta V_{AB}^N = -\Delta P_{AB} \qquad (3.26)$$

If the individual has a nonlinear perception of the amount of money, then the difference of the nonmonetary components at the indifference point can be expressed as

$$\Delta V_{AB}^N = -(U(P_A) - U(P_B)) = U(P_B) - U(P_A) \qquad (3.27)$$

3.5 Methodology of Measuring Nonmonetary Values

It is hard to find the nonmonetary component of value because it is associated with the internal individual perception which is quite subjective. This means that there is no way to find a clear scale and the origin point for such an estimate. However, this task becomes much easy if an individual has to make the choice between two jobs, between two products and any other comparative choice. If the individual has to make a decision on choosing between two or more opportunities – jobs to take, goods to purchase, and any other choice – then it is feasible to find the indifference point for this choice. An individual is offered to choose between two opportunities with given monetary values. The individual makes his choice. It is clear that the individual chooses the opportunity with the highest general value. Then the monetary value of one of the choices varies until the individual becomes indifferent in his choice. At the indifference point, the general values of both choices become equal to the individual, At this point the difference of the nonmonetary values of these choices can be measures by the difference of the monetary values of those choices according to Eq.(3.4). The more detailed relationship between the difference of the nonmonetary and monetary values at the indifference point in case of choosing a job or a making a purchasing decision are presented in Eqs.(3.14), (3.16) for jobs and Eqs.(3.26), (3.27) for buying decisions of consumer goods and services.

Case studies on measuring the nonmonetary component of value are presented in the following chapters.

3.6 Survey Method for Finding the Indifference Point

A survey method is used to identify the indifference point to find the difference of the nonmonetary values of two choices. The survey questionnaire presents two choices – jobs, products, or any two scenarios in decision making. The choices are presented with the various monetary components of values. In case of jobs, the monetary components are presented with different levels of compensation (salaries) for at least on the jobs to compare with another job. In case of products, the monetary components are presented with different levels of prices for at least on the products to compare with another product.

The respondents select one of the jobs according to the suggested compensations for each pair of compensations or indicate that they have no preference. This is the indifference point and the difference of the monetary compensations measures the difference of the nonmonetary values of the jobs for the individual according to Eq.(3.16).

For the purchasing decision, the respondents select one of the products according to the suggested prices or indicate that they have no preference. No preference indicates the indifference point at which the difference of the monetary compensations measures the difference of the nonmonetary values of the product for the individual according to Eq.(3.26).

3.7 The Survey for Job Selection

3.7.1 The Questionnaire for Job Selection

A sample questionnaire is illustrated in Figure 3-5. Respondents were offered to choose between two well-known jobs. One of two jobs in the questionnaire was offered with a fixed monetary compensation while the second job was offered at a variety of compensations. The respondents were asked to indicate their preference between two jobs at each pair of compensations— the fixed compensation for the first job and each compensation option of the second job.

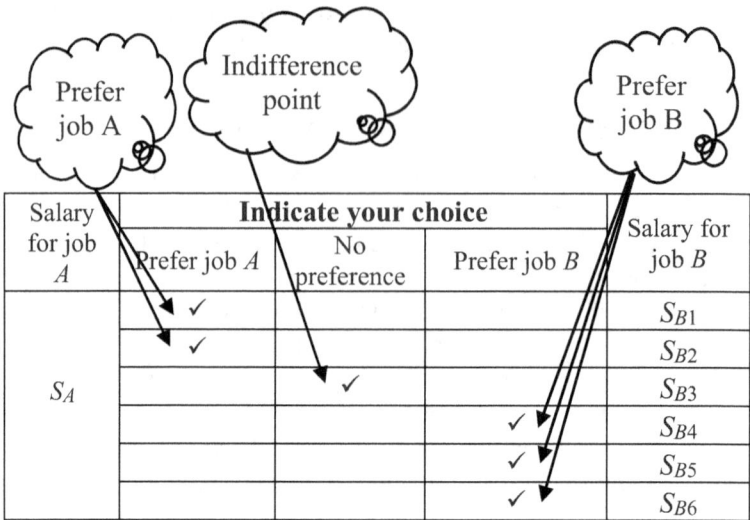

Figure 3-5: A sample questionnaire

For example, the questionnaire in Figure 3-5 offers two jobs, A and B. Job A was offered with a fixed compensation S_A while job B was offered with various compensations, $S_{B1}, \ldots, S_{B6}$. A respondent has to indicate his personal preference by choosing between jobs A and B for each option of the compensation for job B from the list of possible compensations presented in the right column in the questionnaire (Figure 3-5). The choice has to be indicated by a checkmark placed in the appropriate column "Prefer job A", "No preferences" or "Prefer job B". The sample answers shown in Figure 3-5 indicate that the respondent prefers job A (with a fixed compensation S_A) over job B with compensations S_{B1} or S_{B2} for job B. On the other hand, the respondent prefers job B over job A with compensations S_{B4} and higher for job B. However the respondent has no preference between jobs A or B with compensations S_{B3} for job B. Let's refer this choice to as the indifference point. At the indifference point, the difference of the difference of the nonmonetary values of jobs A and B is balanced by the difference of the monetary compensations according to Eq.(3.16).

To avoid confusion of the respondents on how to fill up the questionnaire, each actual questionnaire contained an example of an answer similar to one shown in Figure 3-5.

3 Measuring the Nonmonetary Component of Value   47

Figure 3-6 illustrates the logic of the questionnaire shown in Figure 3-5. In Figure 3-6, the respondent chooses compensation S_{B3} for job B as the indifference point in comparison to job A with compensation S_A. The indifference point means that the difference in compensations,

$$\Delta V_{AB}^M = \Delta S_{AB} = S_{B3} - S_A \qquad (3.28)$$

offsets the difference in nonmonetary values of these two jobs

$$\Delta V_{AB}^N = V_B^N - V_A^N \qquad (3.29)$$

Then at the indifference point and according to Eq.(3.16), the difference of the nonmonetary values of jobs A and B is equal to the negative difference of the monetary values of these jobs, i.e.

$$\Delta V_{AB}^N = -\Delta V_{AB}^M = -\Delta S_{AB} = S_A - S_{B3} \qquad (3.30)$$

Such a condition makes the total general values of both jobs equal.

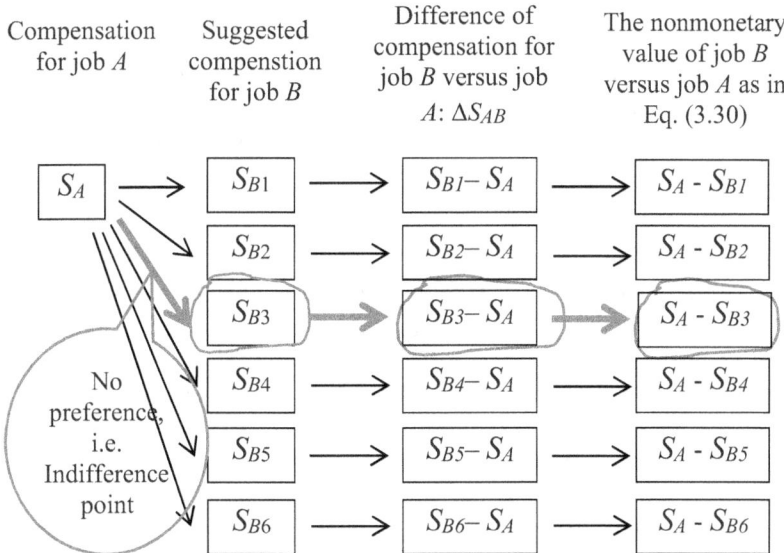

Figure 3-6: The logical schema of the sample questionnaire shown in Figure 3-5

3.7.2 Survey Processing Methodology

All respondents participated in the survey had to fill up the questionnaire. All incomplete or wrongly filled questionnaires, which did not clearly and unambiguously indicate indifference points, were marked as invalid responses and discarded from the further processing. Suppose there are N valid questionnaires left for the processing after discarding the invalid ones. It is natural to expect that different people might have different opinions about the jobs and chose different compensations for job B in the questionnaire as the point of indifference relative to job A. Thus, n_1 respondents chose compensation S_{B1} as the point of indifference between jobs A and B in the questionnaire in Figure 3-5, n_2 respondents chose compensation S_{B2}, n_3 respondents chose S_{B3}, n_4 respondents chose S_{B4}, n_5 respondents chose S_{B5}, n_6 and respondents chose S_{B6}. The total number of valid responses N is equal to the sum of the numbers of the respecive responses n_k as

$$\sum_{k=1}^{6} n_k = N \qquad (3.31)$$

The distribution of the respondents by indifference points chosen by them and the respective differences of the monetary and nonmonetary values of the jobs obtained from N valid questionnaires in the sample survey shown in Figure 3-5 are illustrated in Table 3-1.

The first column in Table 3-1 shows the fixed salary offered with job A and the second column in the table shows a variety of salaries offered with job B. The third column in the table shows the number of respondents, who chose the respective salary of job B as the indifference point. The fourth column shows the relative monetary values (difference of monetary values of the jobs) as the difference of the salaries, and the fifth column shows the calculated relative nonmonetary values (the difference of the nonmonetary values) of the jobs as the opposite of the difference of the monetary values.

3 Measuring the Nonmonetary Component of Value

Table 3-1: Processing of results of a survey conducted with the questionnaire in Figure 3-5

Salary of Job A	Salary of Job B	Number of respondents by indifference points	Difference of monetary values $\Delta V_{AB}^M = S_B - S_A$	Difference of nonmonetary values $\Delta V_{AB}^N = -\Delta V_{AB}^M = S_A - S_B$
S_A	S_{B1}	n_1	$S_{B1} - S_A$	$S_A - S_{B1}$
	S_{B2}	n_2	$S_{B2} - S_A$	$S_A - S_{B2}$
	S_{B3}	n_3	$S_{B3} - S_A$	$S_A - S_{B3}$
	S_{B4}	n_4	$S_{B4} - S_A$	$S_A - S_{B4}$
	S_{B5}	n_5	$S_{B5} - S_A$	$S_A - S_{B5}$
	S_{B6}	n_6	$S_{B6} - S_A$	$S_A - S_{B6}$

According to Table 3-1, the mean difference of the nonmonetary values of jobs A and B on the sample of N respondents can be calculated as

$$\overline{\Delta V_{AB}^N} = \frac{1}{N}\sum_{k=1}^{6}\left(n_k \Delta V_{ABk}^N\right) = \frac{1}{N}\sum_{k=1}^{6}\left(n_k (S_A - S_{Bk})\right) \qquad (3.32)$$

with the standard deviation of the relative nonmonetary value (actually, the difference of nonmonetary values) which can be calculated as

$$\sigma = \frac{1}{N-1}\sum_{k=1}^{6}\left(n_k \left(\Delta V_{ABk}^N - \overline{\Delta V_{AB}^N}\right)^2\right) = \\ = \frac{1}{N-1}\sum_{k=1}^{6}\left(n_k \left((S_A - S_{Bk}) - \overline{\Delta V_{AB}^N}\right)^2\right) \qquad (3.33)$$

3.8 The Survey for Purchasing Decision

3.8.1 The Questionnaire for Purchasing Decision

Survey questionnaires for buying decision are also focused on finding the indifference point between two products or two services for the respondent as shown in a sample in Figure 3-7. The respondents were offered to choose between two well-known products (goods or services), so the respondents had clear understanding of these products. One of two products had a fixed price while the other product was offered at a variety of different prices. The respondents were asked to indicate their preference on what product to buy at each pair of prices.

Fixed Price P_A for good A	Prefer to buy good A	Have no preference – indifference point	Prefer to buy good B	Suggested price P_B for good B
P_A	✓			P_{B1}
	✓			P_{B2}
		✓		P_{B3}
			✓	P_{B4}
			✓	P_{B5}
			✓	P_{B6}

Figure 3-7: A sample questionnaire for buying decisions

For example, the sample questionnaire in Figure 3-7 offers two products, A and B. Product B is offered at various prices $P_{B1} < P_{B2} < P_{B3} < P_{B4} < P_{B5} < P_{A6}$ while product A is offered at a fixed price P_A. These prices are chosen in a such way that the respondents will surely choose product A at price P_{B1} for product B and choose product B at price P_{B6} for product B. A respondent should indicate his personal preference of buying product A or B for each price P_{Bn} for product B from the list of prices in the second column. The sample answers shown in Figure 3-7 indicate that the respondent prefers product A over product B at prices P_{B1} and P_{B2} for product A. On the other hand, the respondent prefers product B over product A at prices P_{B4} and higher for product B. However, the respondent has no preference of buying good A or B at price P_{B3} for product B. Let's refer this choice to as the indifference point. At the indifference point, both products have equal general values for the individual, thus the difference of the nonmonetary values of products A and B are compensated by the difference of prices (monetary value) and can be calculated according to Eq.(3.26).

3 Measuring the Nonmonetary Component of Value

To avoid confusion of the respondents on how to fill up the questionnaire, each actual questionnaire contained an sample answer similar to one shown in Figure 3-7.

Figure 3-8 illustrates the logical schema of the sample questionnaire shown in Figure 3-7. As soon as the respondent comes to the indifference point at price P_{B3} for product B, it means that the difference in prices, i.e. $P_{B3} - P_A$ offsets the difference in nonmonetary values that makes the general values of both products equal in the perception of the respondent. Then according to Eq.(3.26), the difference of the nonmonetary values of product A and B is $P_A - P_{B3}$.

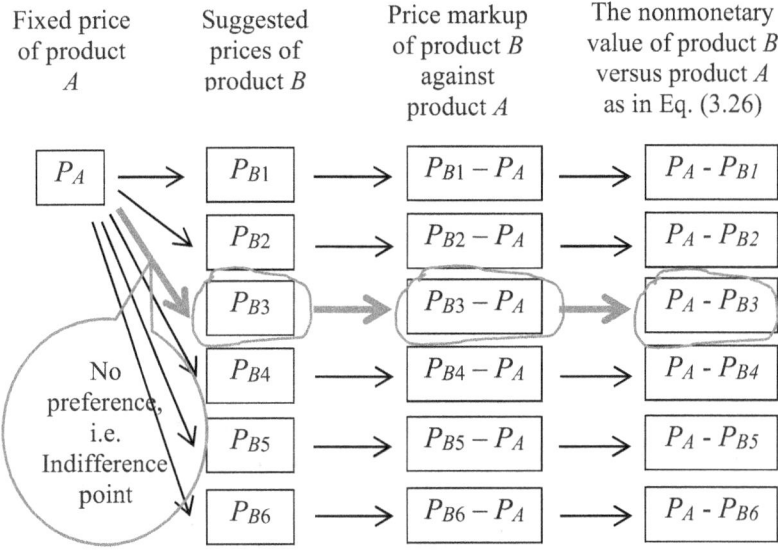

Figure 3-8: The logical schema of the sample questionnaire shown in Figure 3-7

Both rightmost columns in Figure 3-8 look identical but just with opposite signs. However, these two columns present the difference of monetary and nonmonetary values at the indifference point in case of neutral perception of money, $U(P) = P$, in a buying decision. At the indifference point, the difference of nonmonetary values equals the difference in prices (Eq.(3.26)) because in a buying transaction price negatively contributed to the general value. In a more general case, the two rightmost columns in Figure 3-8 may look differently.

3.9 Nonmonetary Values as Perceptual Biase

3.9.1 Perceptual Bias

There are no completely objective humans. Every individual has a perceptual bias to most phenomena, situations, jobs, goods, and services. Each bias causes the nonmonetary component of value.

We will measure the degree of the perceptual bias by the ratio of the nonmonetary component to the monetary component of value,

$$\gamma = \frac{V^N}{V^M} \qquad (3.34)$$

Parameter γ defined in Eq.(3.34) is referred to as **perceptual bias**. The perceptual bias equals zero, if the nonmonetary component is equal to zero. The higher the perceptual bias, the stronger is the individual's subjective attachment or detachment to the given choice.

3.9.2 Relative Perceptual Bias

The difference of nonmonetary values of two different choices depends on the units of measurement. For example, the magnitude of value expressed in dollars or in cents would differ hundred times. A similar effect would appear in comparing nonmonetary values in different countries, which use different currencies, as well as when comparing monthly with annual wages and charges. To make such a difference universally independent of the chosen units of measurement, let's introduce the dimensionless parameter referred to as **relative perceptual bias** and defines as

$$\beta_{AB} = \left(V_B^N - V_A^N\right)/V_A^M \qquad (3.35)$$

Taking into account that the relative perceptual bias is measured at the indifference point, Eq.(3.36) can be rewritten as

$$\beta_{AB} = \left(V_B^N - V_A^N\right)/V_A^M = \Delta V_{AB}^N / V_A^M = -\Delta V_{AB}^M / V_A^M =$$
$$= -\left(V_A^M - V_B^M\right)/V_A^M = \left(P_A - P_B\right)/P_A = -\frac{\Delta P_{AB}}{P_A} \quad (3.36)$$

where prices are given at the indifference point. The relative perceptual bias shows the relative differences of the nonmonetary values of two products, jobs, transactions, or actions versus the monetary value of the reference product, job, transaction, or action, respectively.

4 Measuring Nonmonetary Value of Jobs in San Francisco Bay Area

4.1 Survey Domain and Sampling

The difference of nonmonetary values (relative nonmonetary values) of jobs in terms of employment decision matching the appropriate difference in monetary values (relative monetary values) of the jobs by bringing their general values to the indifference point.

The surveys were conducted in four different social groups including:

- graduate students of the School of Business at Lincoln University, Oakland, CA,
- taxi drivers,
- construction workers, and
- restaurant waiters

in the San Francisco Bay Area, California (Berkeley, Oakland, and San Francisco).

The surveys were conducted separately in four above mentioned social groups. We used various social groups in our research to find out whether there is a difference in the perception and preferences in the assessment of nonmonetary values of the jobs among the different groups of people.

In the surveys, we included jobs of Chief Executive Officer (CEO), financial clerk (FC), and garbage collector (GC). In the survey the respondents were to choose between the CEO and FC jobs, between the CF and GC jobs, as well as between the CEO and GC jobs. To find the indifference points between the jobs, the survey questionnaires offered a wide range of salaries – from reasonable salaries through unrealistically high – for the less attractive jobs to offset their lower nonmonetary value. For example, the salary range for a FC job was offered up to unreasonably high salaries to find an indifference point with a CEO job; a GC job was offered up to unrealistically high salaries to offset its lower nonmonetary value relative to a FC job. The choice between CEO versus GC jobs was added to the survey for consistency to analyze a possible triangular arbitrage for each individual and for the mean assessment in each social group.

All incomplete and wrongly filled questionnaires were disqualified as invalid and removed from the survey pool. The portion of invalid responses varied from 20% through 40% per each survey. In result, the sample sizes of the valid responses for different surveys varied from 130 through 170 as of the number of valid filled questionnaires per survey.

All valid results were collected and statistically processed with the confidence level of 90%.

4.2 The Survey among Business Students of Lincoln University, Oakland, CA

The first survey was conducted among students of Business School at Lincoln University in Oakland, California.

4.2.1 Chief Executive Officer (CEO) vs. Financial Clerk (FC) by Business Students

The first survey was dedicated to the choice between two business positions, Chief Executive Officer (CEO) and Financial Clerk (FC). In the CEO-FC pair, a CEO position was offered in

4 Measuring Nonmonetary Value of Jobs

the questionnaire with the annual compensation of $140K while a financial clerk (FC) position was offered with various compensations as $145K, $155K, $170K, $185K, $195K, and $210K[5]. The respondents had to identify their indifference points by choosing one of the jobs depending on the offered compensations.

The total number of valid responses, i.e., correctly filled and hence qualified questionnaires was 124. The results of the survey on the choice between CEO and FC positions conducted among business students of Lincoln University are shown in Table 4-1.

Table 4-1: Results of the survey on CEO vs. FC jobs conducted among business students

\multicolumn{5}{c}{Nonmonetary Value of CEO vs. FC jobs (among business students)}
Salary of CEO	Salary of FC	Number of respondents	ΔV_{CEO-FC}^{M}	ΔV_{CEO-FC}^{N}
$140K	$145K	6	$5K	-$5K
	$155K	12	$15K	-$15K
	$170K	40	$30K	-$30K
	$185K	32	$45K	-$45K
	$195K	24	$55K	-$55K
	$210K	10	$70K	-$70K

Number of valid responses:	124	
	Relative nonmonetary value	Relative perceptual bias
Mean on sample $\overline{\Delta V_{CEO-FC}^{N}}$:	-$39K	-0.28
Standard deviation:	$17K	0.12

Confidence level:	\multicolumn{2}{c}{90%}
Confidence interval:	±$2K	±0.014
Mean on population:	-$39±2K	-0.28±0.014

---

[5] K means thousand, thus $100K means $100,000

The middle column "Number of respondents" shows the number of respondents who chose the appropriate salary of FC for the indifference point against the CEO job. For example, the first data row of the table shows that 6 respondents chose $145K as a salary for FC at which they have no preference between that job and a job of CEO with the salary of $140K.

According to the results of the survey, the mean relative nonmonetary value of a CEO job versus a FC job on the sample is $39K with the standard deviation of $17K. The confidence interval with the confidence level of 90% is ±$2K that results in the mean relative nonmonetary value of a CEO job versus a FC job on the population as $39K±2K.

Figure 4-1 shows the distribution histogram of the relative nonmonetary value of a chief executive officer (CEO) job versus a financial clerk (FC) job among business students. The dotted curve shows the respective normal distribution of the nonmonetary value for the population of university students with 90% confidence level.

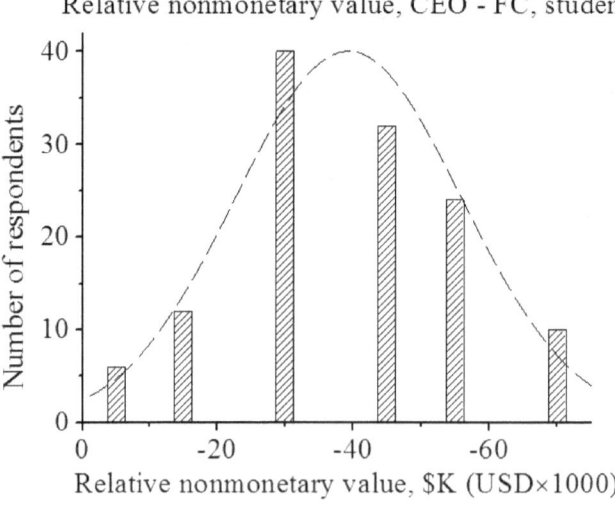

Figure 4-1: The distribution histogram of the relative nonmonetary value of CEO vs. FC jobs among business students. The dashed curve shows the associated normal distribution

4 Measuring Nonmonetary Value of Jobs

4.2.2 Financial Clerk (FC) vs. Garbage Collector (GC) by Business Students

In the same survey among business students of Lincoln University, the respondents were to choose between a financial clerk (FC) and a garbage collector (GC) jobs. In the FC-GC pair, the financial clerk (FC) job was offered in the questionnaire with the annual salary of $50K while a garbage collector (GC) job was offered with a variety of salaries mostly exceeding the compensation for FC to offset the lower nonmonetary value of a GC job against a FC job. The offered salaries for a GC job were $60K, $75K, $80K, $90K, $95K, $110K, and $115K. The respondents were to indicate their preference depending on the offered compensations.

The total number of valid responses in the survey was 124. The results of the survey on the comparison of FC and GC jobs conducted among business students at Lincoln University are shown in Table 4-2.

Table 4-2: Results of the survey on FC vs. GC jobs conducted among business students

Nonmonetary Value of FC vs. GC jobs (among business students)				
Salary of CF	Salary of GC	Number of respondents	ΔV^M_{FC-GC}	ΔV^N_{FC-GC}
$50K	$60K	2	$10K	-$10K
	$75K	27	$25K	-$25K
	$80K	50	$30K	-$30K
	$90K	22	$40K	-$40K
	$95K	15	$45K	-$45K
	$110K	7	$60K	-$60K
	$115K	1	$65K	-$65K

Number of valid responses:	124	
	Relative nonmonetary value	Relative perceptual bias
Mean on sample $\overline{\Delta V^N_{FC-GC}}$:	-$34K	-0.68
Standard deviation:	$10K	0.2

Confidence level:	90%	
Confidence interval:	±$1K	±0.02
Mean on population:	-$34±1K	- 0.68±0.02

The middle column "Number of respondents" in the table shows the number of respondents who chose the appropriate salary of GC as the indifference point against the FC job. For example, the first data row of the table shows that 2 respondents chose $60K as a salary for GC at which they have no preference between that job and a job of FC with the annual salary of $50K.

Figure 4-2 shows the distribution histogram of the relative nonmonetary value of a financial clerk (FC) job versus a garbage collector (GC) job among business students.

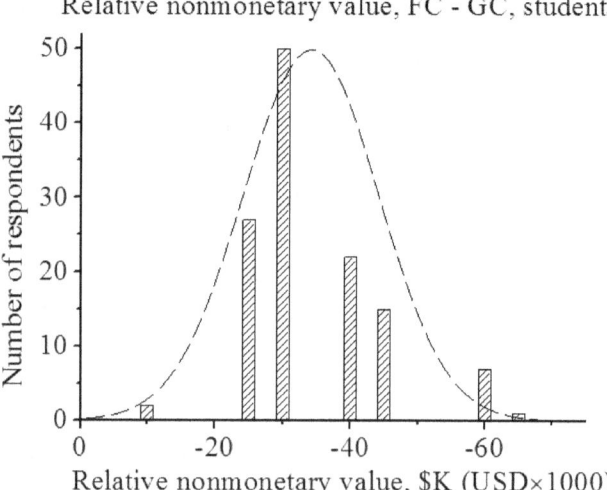

Figure 4-2: The distribution histogram of the relative nonmonetary value of FC vs. GC jobs among business students. The dashed curve shows the associated normal distribution

4.2.3 Chief Executive Officer (CEO) vs. Garbage Collector (GC) by Business Students

Finally, the students were given the choice between two jobs, CEO and GC. The position of CEO was offered at annual salary of $140K while the job of garbage collector (GC) was offered at $155K, $180K, $185K, $195K, $200K, $210K, and $215K which was unrealistically high to offset the nonmonetary status of the CEO job.

Table 4-3: Results of the survey on CEO vs. GC jobs conducted among business students

Nonmonetary Value of CEO vs. GC jobs (among business students)				
Salary of CEO	Salary of GC	Number of respondents	ΔV^M_{CEO-GC}	ΔV^N_{CEO-GC}
$140K	$155K	2	$15K	-$15K
	$180K	3	$40K	-$40K
	$185K	10	$45K	-$45K
	$195K	13	$55K	-$55K
	$200K	17	$60K	-$60K
	$210K	23	$70K	-$70K
	$215K	19	$75K	-$75K

Number of valid responses:	124	
	Relative nonmonetary value	Relative perceptual bias
Mean on sample $\overline{\Delta V^N_{CEO-GC}}$:	-$73K	-0.52
Standard deviation:	$23K	0.16

Confidence level:	90%	
Confidence interval:	±$3K	±0.02
Mean on population:	-$73±3K	-0.52±0.02

The results of the business student choices are shown in Table 4-3. The mean value of the relative nonmonetary value of a

CEO job versus a GC job is $73K±3K assessed with the 90% confidence.

Figure 4-3 shows the distribution histogram of the relative nonmonetary value of a CEO job versus garbage collector (GC) job among business students.

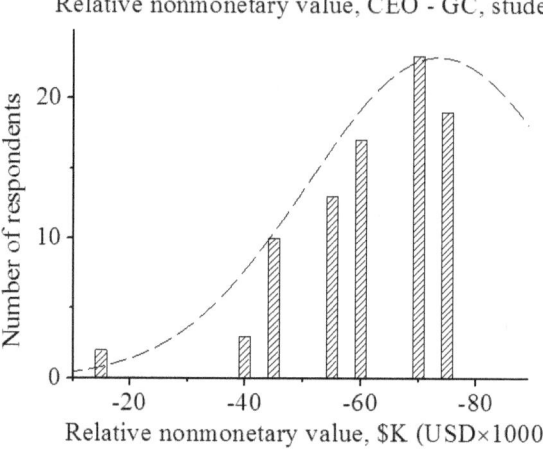

Figure 4-3: The distribution histogram of the relative nonmonetary value of CEO vs. GC jobs among business students. The dashed curve shows the associated normal distribution

Table 4-4: The comparison of the relative nonmonetary values of CEO vs. CF, CF vs. GC, and CEO vs. GC jobs obtained in the survey conducted among business students

Confidence level:	90%	
	Relative nonmonetary values of jobs:	Relative perceptual bias of jobs
ΔV^N_{CEO-FC}	-$39±2K	-0.28±0.014
ΔV^N_{FC-GC}	-$34±1K	-0.68±0.02
ΔV^N_{CEO-GC}	-$73±3K	-0.58±0.02

4 Measuring Nonmonetary Value of Jobs

The comparison of the nonmonetary values obtained in the survey conducted among business students is presented in Table 4-4.

The relative nonmonetary values of the jobs in Table 4-4 show perfect consistency, i.e.

$$\Delta V^N_{CEO-FC} + \Delta V^N_{FC-GC} + \Delta V^N_{GC-CEO} = 0 \tag{4.1}$$

that shows no triangular arbitrage. In Eq.(4.1), we used $\Delta V^N_{GC-CEO} = -\Delta V^N_{CEO-GC}$ in accordance to the anticommutative property of relative value

$$\Delta V^N_{BA} = -\Delta V^N_{AB} \quad \text{and} \quad \Delta S_{BA} = -\Delta S_{AB} \tag{4.2}$$

introduced in Chapter 3, Eq.(3.17).

4.3 The Survey among Taxi Drivers in the Berkeley-Oakland-San Francisco Area

A similar questionnaire with slightly modified amounts of salaries was distributed among taxi drivers from the Berkeley-Oakland-San Francisco area. The respondents were asked about the same choice of jobs, i.e. chief executive officer (CEO), financial clerk (FC) and garbage collector (GC). The total number of valid responses in this survey was 74.

4.3.1 Chief Executive Officer (CEO) vs. Financial Clerk (FC) by Taxi Drivers

In the CEO-FC pair, a CEO position was offered in the questionnaire with the annual salary of $140K while a financial clerk (FC) position was offered with various salaries as $145K, $155K, $170K, $180K, $185K, $195K, $200K, and $210K. The taxi drivers had to check the appropriate boxes to identify their preferences and the indifference points depending on the offered compensations.

The results of the survey regarding the comparison of a CEO and FC positions conducted among taxi drivers are shown in Table 4-5.

Table 4-5: Results of the survey on CEO vs. FC jobs conducted among taxi drivers

Salary of CEO	Nonmonetary Value of CEO vs. FC jobs (among taxi drivers)			
	Salary of FC	Number of respondents	ΔV^{M}_{CEO-FC}	ΔV^{N}_{CEO-FC}
$140K	$145K	4	$5K	-$5K
	$155K	4	$15K	-$15K
	$170K	12	$30K	-$30K
	$180K	28	$40K	-$40K
	$185K	14	$45K	-$45K
	$195K	8	$55K	-$55K
	$200K	2	$60K	-$60K
	$205K	2	$65K	-$65K

Number of valid responses:	74	
	Relative nonmonetary value	Relative perceptual bias
Mean on sample $\overline{\Delta V^{N}_{CEO-FC}}$:	-$39K	-0.28
Standard deviation:	$13K	0.09

Confidence level:	90%	
Confidence interval:	±$2K	±0.01
Mean on population:	-$39±2K	-0.28±0.01

The column "Number of Respondents" in Table 4-5 shows the number of respondents who chose the appropriate pairs of salaries as an indifference point. For example, in the first data row in the table, 4 respondents have no preference between a job of CEO with the annual salary $140K and job of financial clerk if paid $145K annually.

According to the survey (Table 4-5), the mean relative nonmonetary value of a CEO job versus a Financial Clerk job is $39±2K calculated with the confidence level of 90% from 74 valid responses on the sample taxi drivers.

Figure 4-4 shows the distribution histogram of the relative nonmonetary value of a CEO job versus a financial clerk (FC) job in the perception of taxi drivers.

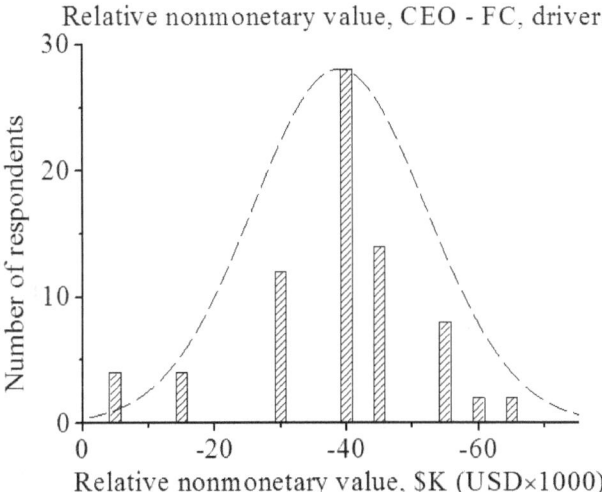

Figure 4-4: The distribution histogram of the relative nonmonetary value of CEO and FC jobs in the perception of taxi drivers. The dashed curve shows the associated normal distribution

4.3.2 Financial Clerk (FC) vs. Garbage Collector (GC) by Taxi Drivers

The same taxi drivers as in the previous case were asked to choose between a financial clerk (FC) and a garbage collector (GC) jobs. In the FC-GC pair of jobs, a financial clerk (FC) job was offered in the questionnaire with the annual salary of $50K while a garbage collector (GC) job was offered with a variety of salaries mostly exceeding the compensation for FC to offset the lower nonmonetary value of a GC job against a FC job. The offered annual salaries for a GC job were $75K, $80K, $90K, $95K, $100K, and $105K. The respondents were to indicate their preferences depending on the offered compensations.

The results of the survey on the comparison of FC and GC jobs conducted among taxi drivers are shown in Table 4-6.

Table 4-6: Results of the survey on FC vs. GC jobs conducted among taxi drivers

Nonmonetary Value of FC vs. GC jobs (among taxi drivers)				
Salary of FC	Salary of GC	Number of respondents	ΔV^M_{FC-GC}	ΔV^N_{FC-GC}
$50K	$75K	4	$25K	-$25K
	$80K	6	$30K	-$30K
	$90K	35	$40K	-$40K
	$95K	18	$45K	-$45K
	$100K	9	$50K	-$50K
	$105K	2	$55K	-$55K

Number of valid responses:	74	
	Relative nonmonetary value	Relative perceptual bias
Mean on sample $\overline{\Delta V^N_{FC-GC}}$:	-$41K	-0.82
Standard deviation:	$7K	0.14

Confidence level:	90%	
Confidence interval:	±$1K	±0.02
Mean on population:	-$41±1K	-0.82±0.02

According to the survey, the mean relative nonmonetary value of a finance clerk (FC) versus a garbage collector (GC) jobs is $41±1K calculated with the confidence factor of 90% on sample of 74 taxi drivers (valid responses).

Figure 4-5 shows the distribution histogram of the relative nonmonetary value of a financial clerk (FC) job versus a garbage collector (GC) job among taxi drivers.

4 Measuring Nonmonetary Value of Jobs

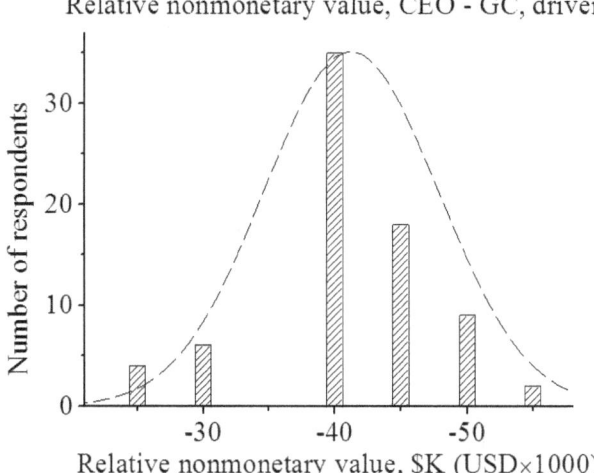

Figure 4-5: The distribution histogram of the relative nonmonetary values of FC vs. GC jobs in the perception of taxi drivers. The dashed curve shows the associated normal distribution

4.3.3 Chief Executive Officer (CEO) vs. Garbage Collector (GC) by Taxi Drivers

Finally, the taxi drivers were given the choice between two jobs, CEO and GC. The position of CEO was offered at annual salary of $140K while the job of garbage collector (GC) was offered at $155K, $180K, $185K, $195K, $200K, $210K, and $215K which was unrealistically high but might offset the nonmonetary status of the CEO job.

The results of the choice made by the taxi drivers are shown in Table 4-7. The mean value of the relative nonmonetary value of a CEO job vs. a (GC) job is $81K±3K with 90% confidence on the sample of 74 taxi drivers.

Table 4-7: Results of the survey on CEO vs. GC jobs conducted among taxi drivers

Nonmonetary Value of CEO vs. GC jobs (among taxi drivers)				
Salary of CEO	Salary of GC	Number of respondents	ΔV^M_{CEO-GC}	ΔV^N_{CEO-GC}
$140K	$185K	4	$45K	-$45K
	$195K	5	$55K	-$55K
	$200K	6	$60K	-$60K
	$210K	8	$70K	-$70K
	$220K	21	$80K	-$80K
	$230K	11	$90K	-$90K
	$235K	9	$95K	-$95K
	$240K	1	$100K	-$100K
	$250K	9	$110K	-$110K

Number of valid responses:	74	
	Relative nonmonetary value	Relative perceptual bias
Mean on sample $\overline{\Delta V^N_{CEO-GC}}$:	-$81K	-0.58
Standard deviation:	$18K	0.13

Confidence level:	90%	
Confidence interval:	±$3K	±0.02
Mean on population:	-$81±3K	-0.58±0.02

Figure 4-6 shows the distribution histogram of the relative nonmonetary value of a chief executive officer (CEO) job versus a garbage collector (GC) job among taxi drivers.

4 Measuring Nonmonetary Value of Jobs   69

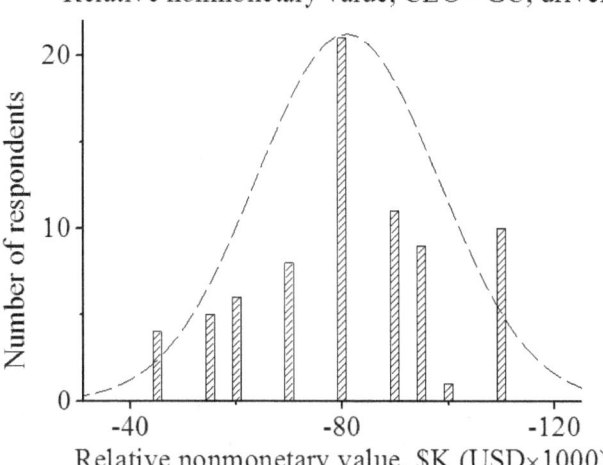

Figure 4-6: The distribution histogram of the relative nonmonetary value of a CEO and a GC jobs in the perception of taxi drivers. The dashed curve shows the associated normal distribution

The comparison of the relative nonmonetary values obtained in the survey conducted among taxi drivers is presented in Table 4-8.

Table 4-8: The comparison of the relative nonmonetary values of CEO vs. FC, FC vs. GC, and CEO vs. GC jobs obtained in the survey conducted among taxi drivers

Confidence level:	90%	
	Relative nonmonetary values of jobs by taxi drivers:	Relative perceptual bias of jobs
ΔV_{CEO-FC}^{N}	-$39±2K	-0.28±0.01
ΔV_{FC-GC}^{N}	-$41±1K	-0.82±0.02
ΔV_{CEO-GC}^{N}	-$81±3K	-0.58±0.02

The relative nonmonetary values of the jobs in the perception of taxi drivers as in Table 4-9 show perfect consistency, i.e.

$$\Delta V^N_{CEO-FC} + \Delta V^N_{FC-GC} + \Delta V^N_{GC-CEO} = -39 - 41 + 81 = 1 \qquad (4.3)$$

that shows practically no triangular arbitrage within the confidence intervals. In Eq.(4.3), we used $\Delta V^N_{GC-CEO} = -\Delta V^N_{CEO-GC}$ in accordance to the anticommutative property of relative value presented in Eq.(4.2).

4.4 Survey among Construction Workers in Berkeley-Oakland-San Francisco Area

The similar surveys were conducted among construction workers from Berkeley, Oakland, and San Francisco. They were given a task of identifying their preferences and the indifference points for the same pairs of jobs including chief executive officer (CEO), financial clerk (FC), and garbage collector (GC). The total number of valid responses in this survey was 77.

4.4.1 Chief Executive Officer (CEO) vs. Financial Clerk (FC) by Construction Workers

In the CEO-FC pair, a CEO position was offered in the questionnaire with the annual salary of $140K while a financial clerk (FC) position was offered with various salaries as $145K, $155K, $170K, $175K, $185K, $195K, and $210K. The construction workers had to check the appropriate boxed to identify their indifference points.

The results of the survey on the comparison of a CEO and FC positions conducted among construction workers are shown in Table 4-9.

4 Measuring Nonmonetary Value of Jobs

Table 4-9: Results of the survey on CEO vs. FC jobs conducted among construction workers

Nonmonetary Value of CEO vs. FC jobs (among construction workers)				
Salary of CEO	Salary of FC	Number of respondents	ΔV_{CEO-FC}^{M}	ΔV_{CEO-FC}^{N}
$140K	$145K	3	$5K	-$5K
	$155K	5	$15K	-$15K
	$170K	9	$30K	-$30K
	$175K	17	$35K	-$35K
	$185K	29	$45K	-$45K
	$195K	6	$55K	-$55K
	$210K	8	$70K	-$70K

Number of valid responses:	77	
	Relative nonmonetary value	Relative perceptual bias
Mean on sample $\overline{\Delta V_{CEO-FC}^{N}}$:	-$41K	-0.29
Standard deviation:	$15K	0.1

Confidence level:	90%	
Confidence interval:	±$3K	±0.02
Mean on population:	-$41±3K	-0.29±0.02

According to the survey (Table 4-9), the mean relative nonmonetary value of a CEO job versus a Financial Clerk job is -$41±3K calculated with the confidence level of 90% on the sample of 77 construction workers.

Figure 4-7 shows the distribution histogram of the relative nonmonetary value of a CEO job versus a financial clerk (FC) job in the perception of construction workers.

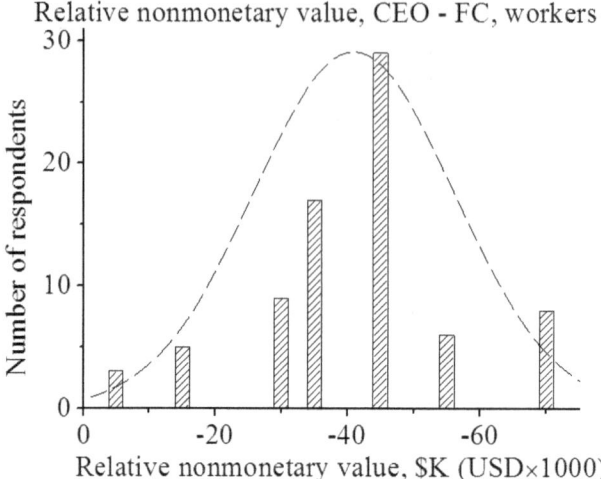

Figure 4-7: The distribution histogram of the relative nonmonetary value of CEO and FC jobs in the perception of construction workers. The dashed curve shows the associated normal distribution

4.4.2 Financial Clerk (FC) vs. Garbage Collector (GC) by Construction Workers

The same construction workers as in the previous case were to choose between a financial clerk (FC) and a garbage collector (GC) jobs. In the FC-GC pair, a financial clerk (FC) job was offered in the questionnaire with the annual salary of $50K while a garbage collector (GC) job was offered with a variety of salaries mostly exceeding the compensation for FC to offset the lower nonmonetary value of a GC job against a FC job. The offered annual salaries for a GC job were $65K, $70K, $75K, $80K, $90K, $95K, $100K, and $105K. The respondents were to indicate their preferences depending on the offered compensations.

The results of the survey on the comparison of FC and GC jobs conducted among construction workers are shown in Table 4-10.

4 Measuring Nonmonetary Value of Jobs 73

Table 4-10: Results of the survey on FC vs. GC jobs conducted among construction workers

Nonmonetary Value of FC vs. GC jobs (among construction workers)				
Salary of CF	Salary of GC	Number of respondents	ΔV_{FC-GC}^{M}	ΔV_{FC-GC}^{N}
$50K	$60K	1	$10K	-$10K
	$70K	2	$20K	-$20K
	$75K	15	$25K	-$25K
	$80K	19	$30K	-$30K
	$90K	18	$40K	-$40K
	$95K	16	$45K	-$45K
	$100K	5	$60K	-$60K
	$105K	1	$65K	-$65K

Number of valid responses:	77	
	Relative nonmonetary value	Relative perceptual bias
Mean on sample $\overline{\Delta V_{FC-GC}^{N}}$:	-$36K	-0.72
Standard deviation:	$11K	0.22

Confidence level:	90%	
Confidence interval:	±$2K	±0.04
Mean on population:	-$36±2K	-0.72±0.04

According to the survey, the mean relative nonmonetary value of a finance clerk (FC) versus a garbage collector (GC) jobs is -$36±2K calculated with the confidence factor of 90% on the sample of 77 construction workers.

Figure 4-8 shows the distribution histogram of the relative nonmonetary value of a financial clerk (FC) job versus a garbage collector (GC) job among construction workers.

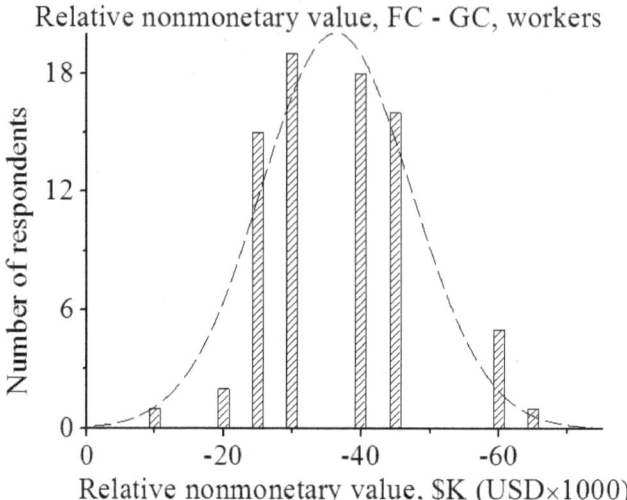

Figure 4-8: The distribution histogram of the relative nonmonetary values of FC vs. GC jobs in the perception of construction workers. The dashed curve shows the associated normal distribution

4.4.3 Chief Executive Officer (CEO) vs. Garbage Collector (GC) by Construction Workers

Finally, the construction workers were given the choice between two jobs, CEO and GC. The position of CEO was offered at annual salary of $140K while the job of garbage collector (GC) was offered at $165K, $175K, $185K, $195K, $200K, $205K, $210K, $215K, $230K, $240K, $245K, $250K, and $255K which were unrealistically high in the expectation to offset the nonmonetary status of the CEO job.

The results of the choices made by the construction workers are shown in Table 4-11. The mean relative nonmonetary value of a CEO job vs. a (GC) job is $77±3K with 90% confidence on the sample of 77 construction workers.

Table 4-11: Results of the survey on CEO vs. GC jobs conducted among construction workers

Salary of CEO	Salary of GC	Number of respondents	ΔV^M_{CEO-GC}	ΔV^N_{CEO-GC}
$140K	$165K	1	$25K	-$25K
	$175K	1	$35K	-$35K
	$185K	3	$45K	-$45K
	$195K	4	$55K	-$55K
	$200K	6	$60K	-$60K
	$205K	7	$65K	-$65K
	$210K	15	$70K	-$70K
	$215K	17	$75K	-$75K
	$230K	6	$90K	-$90K
	$240K	5	$100K	-$100K
	$245K	2	$105K	-$105K
	$250K	1	$110K	-$110K
	$255K	9	$115K	-$115K

Number of valid responses:	77	
	Relative nonmonetary value	Relative perceptual bias
Mean on sample $\overline{\Delta V^N_{CEO-GC}}$:	-$77K	-0.55
Standard deviation:	$21K	0.15

Confidence level:	90%	
Confidence interval:	±$3K	±0.02
Mean on population:	-$77±3K	-0.55±0.02

Figure 4-9 shows the distribution histogram of the relative nonmonetary value of a chief executive officer (CEO) job versus a garbage collector (GC) job among construction workers.

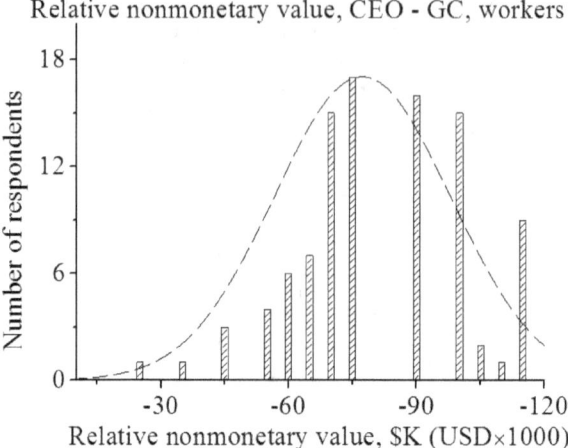

Figure 4-9: The distribution histogram of the relative nonmonetary value of a CEO and a GC jobs in perception of construction workers. The dashed curve shows the associated normal distribution

The comparison of the nonmonetary values obtained in the survey conducted among construction workers is presented in Table 4-12.

Table 4-12: The comparison of the relative nonmonetary values of CEO vs. FC, FC vs. GC, and CEO vs. GC jobs obtained in the survey conducted among construction workers

Confidence level:	90%	
	Relative nonmonetary values of jobs by construction workers	Relative perceptual bias of jobs
ΔV^N_{CEO-FC}	-$41±3K	-0.29±0.02
ΔV^N_{FC-GC}	-$36±2K	-0.72±0.04
ΔV^N_{CEO-GC}	-$77±3K	-0.55±0.02

The relative nonmonetary values of the jobs in the perception of construction workers in Table 4-12 show perfect consistency, i.e.

4 Measuring Nonmonetary Value of Jobs

$$\Delta V^N_{CEO-FC} + \Delta V^N_{FC-GC} + \Delta V^N_{GC-CEO} = -41 - 36 + 77 = 0 \quad (4.4)$$

Eq.(4.4) shows no triangular arbitrage. In Eq.(4.4), we used $\Delta V^N_{GC-CEO} = -\Delta V^N_{CEO-GC}$ in accordance to the anticommutative property of the relative value presented in Eq.(4.2).

4.5 Survey among Restaurant Waiters

The waiters from different restaurants in San Francisco Downtown area participated in the survey. They were given the choice of same three pairs of jobs. The total number of valid responses in this survey was 72.

4.5.1 Chief Executive Officer (CEO) vs. Financial Clerk (FC) by Restaurant Waiters

In the CEO-FC pair of jobs, a CEO position was offered in the questionnaire with the annual salary of $140K while a financial clerk (FC) position was offered with various salaries as $145K, $155K, $160K, $170K, $180K, and $190K. The construction workers had to check the appropriate boxed to identify their indifference points.

The results of the survey on the comparison of a CEO and FC positions conducted among restaurant waiters are shown in Table 4-13.

Table 4-13: Results of the survey on CEO vs. FC jobs conducted among restaurant waiters

	Nonmonetary Value of CEO vs. FC jobs (among restaurant waiters)			
Salary of CEO	Salary of FC	Number of respondents	ΔV^M_{CEO-FC}	ΔV^N_{CEO-FC}
$140K	$145K	8	$5K	-$5K
	$155K	9	$15K	-$15K
	$160K	17	$25K	-$25K
	$170K	20	$30K	-$30K
	$180K	12	$40K	-$40K
	$190K	6	$50K	-$50K

Number of valid responses:	72	
	Relative nonmonetary value	Relative perceptual bias
Mean on sample $\overline{\Delta V^N_{CEO-FC}}$:	-$27K	-0.19
Standard deviation:	$12K	0.09

Confidence level:	90%	
Confidence interval:	±$2K	±0.014
Mean on population:	-$27±2K	-0.19±0.014

According to the survey the mean relative nonmonetary value of a CEO job versus a Financial Clerk job is -$27±2K calculated with the confidence level of 90% on the sample of 72 restaurant waiters.

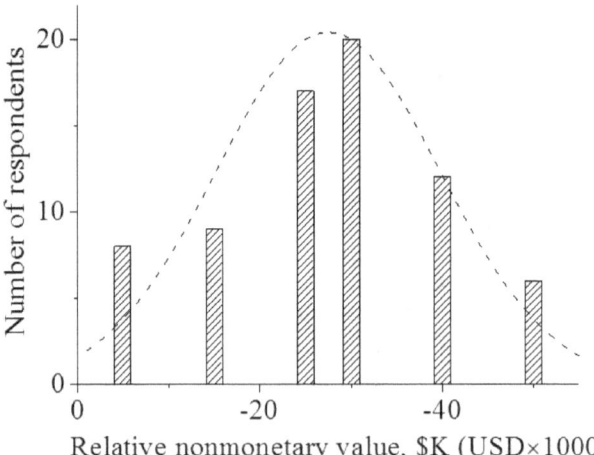

Figure 4-10: The distribution histogram of the relative nonmonetary value of CEO and FC jobs in the perception of restaurant waiters. The dashed curve shows the associated normal distribution

Figure 4-10 shows the distribution histogram of the relative nonmonetary value of a CEO job versus a financial clerk (FC) job in the perception of restaurant waiters.

4.5.2 Survey among Financial Clerk (FC) vs. Garbage Collector (GC) by Restaurant Waiters

The restaurant waiters were also asked to choose between a financial clerk (FC) and a garbage collector (GC) jobs. In the FC-GC pair, a financial clerk (FC) job was offered in the questionnaire with the annual salary of $50K while a garbage collector (GC) job was offered with a variety of salaries mostly exceeding the compensation for FC to offset the lower nonmonetary value of a GC job against a FC job. The offered annual salaries for a GC job were $65K, $85K, $90, $100K, $105, and $110K. The respondents were to indicate their preferences depending on the offered compensations.

The results of the survey on the comparison of FC and GC jobs conducted among construction workers are shown in Table 4-14.

Table 4-14: Results of the survey on FC vs. GC jobs conducted among construction workers

Nonmonetary Value of FC vs. GC jobs (among restaurant waiters)				
Salary of FC	Salary of GC	Number of respondents	ΔV^{M}_{FC-GC}	ΔV^{N}_{FC-GC}
$50K	$65K	7	$15K	-$15K
	$85K	6	$35K	-$35K
	$90K	41	$40K	-$40K
	$100K	12	$50K	-$50K
	$105K	4	$55K	-$55K
	$110K	2	$60K	-$60K

Number of valid responses:	72	
	Relative nonmonetary value	Relative perceptual bias
Mean on sample ΔV^{N}_{FC-GC} :	-$40K	-0.8

Standard deviation:	$10K	0.2

Confidence level:	90%	
Confidence interval:	±$2K	±0.04
Mean on population:	-$40±2K	-0.8±0.04

According to the survey, the mean relative nonmonetary value of a finance clerk (FC) versus a garbage collector (GC) jobs is -$40±2K calculated with the confidence factor of 90% on the sample of 72 restaurant waiters.

Figure 4-11 shows the distribution histogram of the relative nonmonetary value of a financial clerk (FC) job versus a garbage collector (GC) job among restaurant waiters along with the matching normal distribution (a dashed curve) with the mean of -$40K and standard deviation of $10K.

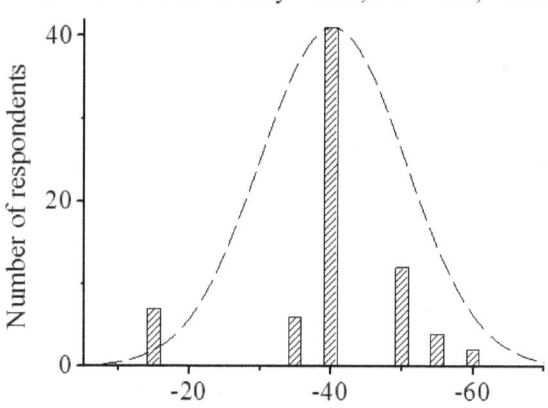

Figure 4-11: The distribution histogram of the relative nonmonetary values of FC vs. GC jobs in the perception of restaurant waiters. The dashed curve shows the associated normal distribution

4.5.3 Chief Executive Officer (CEO) vs. Garbage collector (GC) by Restaurant Waiters

Finally, the restaurant waiters were given the choice between two jobs, CEO and GC. The position of CEO was offered at annual salary of $140K while the job of garbage collector (GC) was offered at $185K, $195K, $205K, $220K, $245K, and $250K which was unrealistically high but might offset the nonmonetary status of the CEO job.

The results of the choices made by the construction workers are shown in Table 4-15. The mean value of the nonmonetary value of a CEO job vs. a (GC) job is -$68±3K with 90% confidence on the sample of 72 restaurant waiters.

Table 4-15: Results of the survey on CEO vs. GC jobs conducted among restaurant waiters

Nonmonetary Value of CEO vs. GC jobs (among restaurant waiters)				
Salary of CEO	Salary of GC	Number of respondents	ΔV_{CEO-GC}^{M}	ΔV_{CEO-GC}^{N}
$140K	$185K	10	$45K	-$45K
	$195K	14	$55K	-$55K
	$205K	23	$65K	-$65K
	$220K	19	$80K	-$80K
	$245K	4	$105K	-$105K
	$250K	2	$110K	-$110K

Number of valid responses:	72	
	Relative nonmonetary value	Relative perceptual bias
Mean on sample $\overline{\Delta V_{CEO-GC}^{N}}$:	-$68K	-0.49
Standard deviation:	$17K	0.12

Confidence level:	90%	
Confidence interval:	±$3K	±0.02
Mean on population:	-$68±3K	-0.49±0.02

Figure 4-12 shows the distribution histogram of the relative nonmonetary value of a chief executive officer (CEO) job versus a garbage collector (GC) job among restaurant waiters with the mean of -$68±3K and standard deviation of $17K.

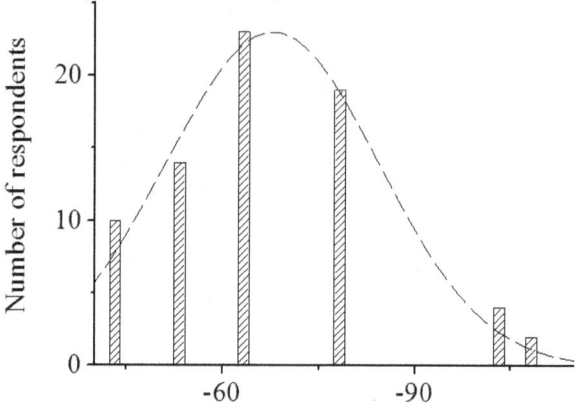

Figure 4-12: The distribution histogram of the relative nonmonetary value of a CEO and a GC jobs in perception of restaurant waiters. The dashed curve shows the associated normal distribution

The comparison of the relative nonmonetary values obtained in the survey conducted among restaurant waiters is presented in Table 4-16.

The relative nonmonetary values of the jobs in the perception of construction workers in Table 4-16 show excellent consistency, i.e.

$$\Delta V^N_{CEO-FC} + \Delta V^N_{FC-GC} + \Delta V^N_{GC-CEO} = -27 - 40 + 68 = 1 \qquad (4.5)$$

that shows no arbitrage within the confidence intervals. In Eq.(4.5), we used $\Delta V^N_{GC-CEO} = -\Delta V^N_{CEO-GC}$ in accordance to the anticommutative property of relative value presented in Eq.(4.2).

Table 4-16: The comparison of the relative nonmonetary values of CEO vs. FC, FC vs. GC, and CEO vs. GC jobs obtained in the survey conducted among restaurant waiters

Confidence level:	90%	
	Relative nonmonetary values of jobs by restaurant waiters:	Relative perceptual bias of jobs
ΔV^N_{CEO-FC}	-$27±2K	-0.19±0.014
ΔV^N_{FC-GC}	-$40±2K	-0.8±0.04
ΔV^N_{CEO-GC}	-$68±3K	-0.49±0.02

4.6 Analysis of the Results by all Group of Respondents

All measured relative nonmonetary values as well as the relative perceptual bias of the jobs assessed in the survey are presented in the aggregate form in Table 4-17.

Table 4-17: Aggregate table for the relative nonmonetary values of jobs

Categories of respondents	Relative nonmonetary values of jobs	ΔV^N_{CEO-FC}	ΔV^N_{FC-GC}	ΔV^N_{CEO-GC}
Business students	Nonmonetary value	-$39±2K	-$34±1K	-$73±3K
	Relative perceptual bias	-0.28±0.014	-0.82±0.02	-0.58±0.02
Taxi drivers	Nonmonetary value	-$39±2K	-$41±1K	-$81±3K
	Relative perceptual bias	-0.28±0.01	-0.82±0.02	-0.58±0.02
Construction workers	Nonmonetary value	-$41±3K	-$36±2K	-$77±3K
	Relative perceptual bias	-0.29±0.02	-0.72±0.04	-0.55±0.02
Restaurant waiters	Nonmonetary value	-$27±2K	-$40±2K	-$68±3K
	Relative perceptual bias	-0.19±0.014	-0.8±0.04	-0.49±0.02

As evident from Table 4-17 above, the mean relative nonmonetary value (the difference in nonmonetary values) for a CEO against a FC jobs is the highest for the construction workers and least for the restaurant waiters. Similarly, the mean relative nonmonetary value of an FC job against GC job is found to be highest for the taxi drivers, and lowest for the business students. Finally, the mean relative nonmonetary value of a CEO job against a GC job was found the highest for the taxi drivers lowest for the restaurant workers.

As follows from Table 4-17 above, all four groups of respondents showed quite similar mean relative perceptual bias for all pairs of jobs regardless of the respondent group. An interesting observation was that the relative perceptual bias for Financial Clerk (FC) versus Garbage Collector (GC) was greater than for the pair of Chief Executive Officer (CEO) versus Garbage Collector (GC). It may be explained as the CEO job required specific skills and talents that was far beyond the respondent groups and therefor was no as attractive for them.

The survey showed good consistency of the measured relative nonmonetary values among various social groups of respondents. Also, the results show good assessment transitivity, i.e.

$$\Delta V^N_{CEO-GC} = \Delta V^N_{CEO-FC} + \Delta V^N_{FC-GC} \qquad (4.6)$$

which was very good in each category of respondents. The assessment of the relative nonmonetary values of a chief executive officer (CEO) job against a garbage collector (GC) in all four surveys was very close to the sum of the relative nonmonetary values of a chief executive officer (CEO) job against a financial clerk (FC) job and a financial clerk (FC) job against a garbage collector (GC) as shown in Table 4-18 and Eqs.(4.3)-(4.6).

The consistency of the survey results presented above in this chapter and collected in the aggregate form in Table 4-18 clearly support the validity of the indifference point method for measuring the nonmonetary component of general value.

4.7 Discussion on the Job Selection Survey

In this chapter, the concept of general value was applied for selection of jobs based on the methodology of finding the indifference point. According to the concept of general value, value is composed of two components: monetary and nonmonetary (Aityan et al., 2016). Both components play an equally important role in the value assessment and decision making. In the today's world, most people still view value through the prism of money only. Considering money alone or its perception is not enough for the assessment of value as was clearly illustrated and described in the chapter using the concept of general value. The nonmonetary component of value is specific to an individual or to a social group.

The nonmonetary component of general value is often referred to as the nonmonetary value. These two terms are completely synonymous.

The most important role in assessment, decision making, and trading is played by the difference of values rather than by the absolute level of value. Thus, measuring the difference of nonmonetary value between any two entities is more important than measuring the absolute level of the nonmonetary value. The difference of the nonmonetary values between two entities is referred to as a relative nonmonetary value. This is similar to the notion of potential energy in physics where only the difference (gradient) of potential energies makes real sense in motion while the absolute value of the potential energy is just a purely theoretical concept.

The methodology for measuring the relative nonmonetary value is based on finding the indifference point. The indifference point is the situation when an individual is neutral in choosing between two entities or between two action scenarios. The indifference point takes place when the general values of the choices are equal. In the indifference point, the relative nonmonetary value (difference of the nonmonetary values) of two choices is equal to the difference of the monetary values of these choices with the opposite sign as indicated in Eq.(3.30) of Chapter 3.

We conducted surveys to measure relative nonmonetary value of different jobs (chief executive officer (CEO), financial clerk (FC), and garbage collector (GC)) in the perception of different social groups of people (business students, taxi drivers, construction workers, and restaurant waiters) with the sample sizes varying from 72 to 124 valid responses per survey. The measured relative nonmonetary values of jobs are very consistent inside the groups and between the groups, and meet the transitivity rule stated in Eq.(4.6) and showed practically no triangular arbitrage of the mean relative nonmonetary value.

The introduced method of measuring relative nonmonetary values turns the theory of general value from a powerful theoretical concept to a practical approach in the assessment of decision making by individuals and groups of people.

5 Measuring Nonmonetary Value of Jobs in Europe

5.1 The Surveys on Job Selection in Europe

The previous chapter discussed the surveys on measuring the nonmonetary values of jobs conducted in the San Francisco Bay Area, California, USA. This chapter discusses similar surveys conducted in two European countries – Germany and Russia. The same methodology of finding the indifference points was used in the European surveys as in the surveys conducted in the USA. The survey methodology and the questionnaire were presented in Chapter 3.

5.2 The Survey on Nonmonetary Value of Jobs in Germany

This survey on nonmonetary value of jobs was conducted among university students in Berlin, Germany. The indifference points were found for the respondents in the comparison of the following jobs: Editor-in-Chief (EiC) and Garbage Collector (GC). The difference of the nonmonetary values of these jobs were measured by the difference of the monetary components of the jobs in the indifference points.

5.2.1 Editor-in-Chief (EiC) vs Garbage Collector (GC) Jobs

The survey participants were presented a questionnaire with the choice between two jobs – Editor-in-chief (EiC) for a multimedia outlet versus Garbage Collector (GC). The monthly salary[6] for EiC job was set to ten thousand Euro (€10K) and the monthly salary for GC was varied from €2K through €30K. The respondents should choose between these two jobs based on the salaries. The difference in the salaries, when the respondents had no preference of the jobs, indicated their indifference points, i.e. the situation of equal general values of both jobs.

The total number of randomly selected participants in the survey was 211. Among all, 14 questionnaires (7% of all presented questionnaires) had corrections or errors. Those 14 questionnaires were rejected as invalid and removed from the pool. Thus, the final number of the accepted filled questionnaires was 197.

5.2.2 The Survey Results for EiC vs GC

The results of the survey are presented in Table 5-1. None of the respondents chose the GC job with the monthly salaries below €15 versus the EiC job with the monthly salary of €10.

Table 5-1: Results of the survey on EiC vs. GC jobs conducted among students in Germany

Nonmonetary Value of EiC vs. GC jobs (among students in Germany)				
Salary of Editor-in-Chief (EiC)	Monthly salary of Garbage Collector (GC)	Number of respondents (Indifference point)	$\Delta V^M_{EiC-GC} = S_{GC} - S_{EiC}$	$\Delta V^N_{EiC-GC} = S_{EiC} - S_{GC}$
€10K	€2K	0	-€8K	€8K
	€5K	0	-€5K	€5K

---

[6] It is typical for the European countries to show monthly salary rather than the annual salary as in the USA.

€8K	0	-€2K	€2K
€10K	0	€0K	€0K
€13K	0	€3K	-€3K
€15K	20	€5K	-€5K
€17K	35	€7K	-€7K
€20K	50	€10K	-€10K
€25K	78	€15K	-€15K
€30K	14	€20K	-€20K

Number of valid responses:	197	
	Relative nonmonetary value	Relative perceptual bias
Mean on sample $\overline{\Delta V^N_{EiC-GC}}$:	-€12K	-1.16
Standard deviation:	€4K	0.4

Confidence level:	90%	
Confidence interval:	±€0.5K	±0.05
Mean on population:	-€12±0.5K	-1.16±0.05

The third column in Table 5-1 shows the number of respondents for whom the indicated difference in salaries of EiC and GC resulted in "no preference" of the job, i.e. caused the indifference point in their decision on the job selection.

The difference in the salaries (the monetary component of general value) at the indifference point (the fourth column in Table 5-1) indicates the same difference in the nonmonetary values of the jobs with the negatie sign (the fifth column in Table 5-1).

According to the survey (Table 5-1), the mean relative nonmonetary value of the Editor-in-Chief (EiC) vs. Garbage Collector (GC) job is -€12±0.5K calculated with the 90% confidence level on the sample of 197 students.

The results of the survey showed that the relative non-monetary bias related to the job of garbage collector (GC) relative to the job of Editor-in-Chief is about -116% that means that the GC job is more than two times less prestigious than the EiC job.

Figure 5-1 shows the distribution of the relative nonmonetary value of a Editor-in-Chief job versus a Garbage Collector job in the perception of German students.

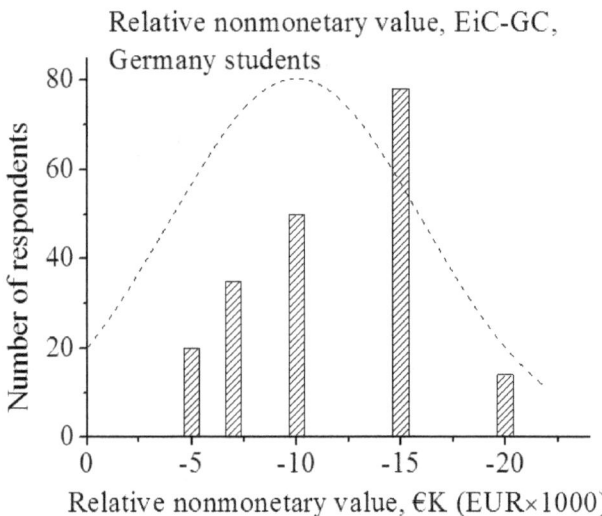

Figure 5-1: The distribution histogram of the relative nonmonetary value of the Editor-in-Chief (EiC) job versus a Garbage Collector (GC) job in the perception of students in Germany. The dashed curve shows the respective normal distribution

The results presented in Table 5-1 and Figure 5-1 indicate that with the little difference in salaries, students prefer the job of Editor-in Chief (GC) because of its higher nonmonetary value. However, as the salary of Garbage Collector (GC) becomes significantly higher than the salary of the Editor-in-Chief (EiC), more students prefer the Garbage Collector (GC) job because its monetary value compensate or exceeds the non monetary value of the Editor-in-Chief job.

5.3 The Survey on Nonmonetary Value of Jobs in Russia

This survey on nonmonetary value of jobs was conducted in 2016 among undergraduate and graduate students at Moscow State Institute of Foreign Affairs (MGIMO) in Moscow, Russia. The indifference points were found for the respondents in the comparison of the following jobs: Senior Manager (SM) and garbage collector (GC). The difference of the nonmonetary values of these jobs were measured by the difference of the monetary components of the jobs in the indifference points.

5.3.1 Senior Manager (SM) vs Garbage Collector (GC) Jobs

The survey participants were presented a questionnaire with the choice between two jobs – Senior Manager (SM) versus Garbage Collector (GC). The monthly salary[7] for SM job was set to two hundred fifty thousand Rubbles (₽250K) and the monthly salary for GC was varied from ₽30K through ₽600K [8]. The respondents should choose between these two jobs based on the salaries. The difference in the salaries, when the respondents had no preference of the jobs, indicated their indifference points, i.e. equal general value of both jobs.

The total number of randomly selected participants in the survey was 100. Some of the questionnaires were filled incorrectly and disqualified as invalid. There were totally 22 invalid questionnaires. The invalid questionnaires were removed from the pool. Thus, the total number of the accepted filled questionnaires was 78.

5.3.2 The Survey Results for SM vs GC

The results of the survey among MGIMO students in Moscow on the nonmonetary value of Senior Manager (SM) and Garbage Collector (GC) jobs are presented in Table 5-2 and Figure 5-2.

---

[7] It is typical to show monthly salary in Russia rather than the annual salary as in the USA.

[8] The exchange rate between US dollar and Russian ruble at the time of the survey was $1 = ₽70.

Table 5-2: Results of the survey on SM vs. GC conducted among Moscow students

Nonmonetary Value of SM vs. GC jobs (among students in Moscow)				
Salary of Senior Manager (SM)	Salary of Garbage Collector (GC)	Number of respondents at the indifference point	ΔV^M_{SM-GC}	ΔV^N_{SM-GC}
₽250K	₽30K	0	-₽220K	₽220K
	₽90K	0	-₽160K	₽160K
	₽150K	0	-₽100K	₽100K
	₽250K	7	₽0K	₽0K
	₽300K	14	₽50K	-₽50K
	₽350K	16	₽100K	-₽100K
	₽400K	12	₽150K	-₽150K
	₽450K	8	₽200K	-₽200K
	₽500K	5	₽250K	-₽250K
	₽550K	9	₽300K	-₽300K
	₽600K	7	₽350K	-₽350K

Number of valid responses:	78	
	Relative nonmonetary value	Relative perceptual bias
Mean on sample $\overline{\Delta V^N_{SM-GC}}$:	-₽155K	-0.62
Standard deviation:	₽107K	0.43

Confidence level:	90%	
Confidence interval:	±₽20K	±0.08
Mean on population:	-₽155±20K	-0.62±0.08

According to the survey (см. Table 5-2), the mean relative nonmonetary value of a Senior Manager vs. Garbage Collector job is -₽155±20K calculated with the confidence level of 90% on the sample of 78 Moscow students.

5 Measuring Nonmonetary Value of Jobs

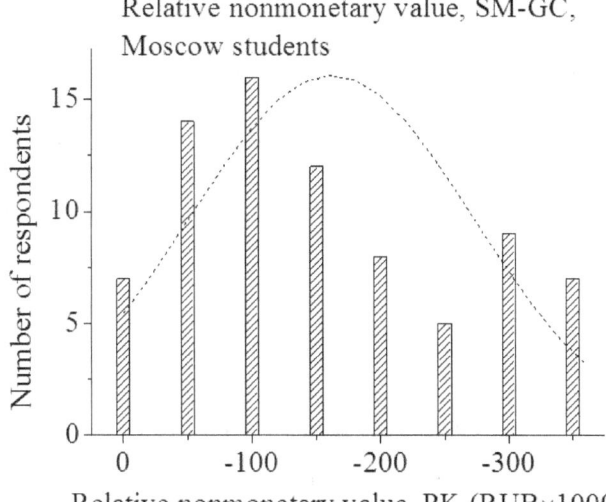

Figure 5-2: The distribution histogram of the relative nonmonetary value of Senior Manager (SM) job versus a Garbage Collector (GC) job in the perception of students in Moscow, Russia. The dashed curve shows the respective normal distribution

Figure 5-2 shows two peaks on the distribution histogram. On one hand, almost 20% of the respondents from the MGIMO students were ready to reject a higher prestige job of senior manager in favor of a lower prestige job of garbage collector with an additional salary of 50 thousand rubles per month. On the other hand, 9% of the respondents were not ready to give up the higher social status job of senior manager even with the difference in salaries of 350 thousand rubles, which is 140% higher than the salary of the senior manager. This may indicate that the sample group may have differences in opinions about the nonmonetary values of jobs. The two peaks in the distribution in Figure 5-2 may represent two distinct groups of students as of their perception of the job prestige versus compensation for it.

Nevertheless, the survey has clearly demonstrated the nonmonetary value of the senior manager (SM) job was for MGIMO students on average by 155 thousand rubles monthly salary higher than the job of garbage collector (GC).

The results of the surveys on nonmonetary value of jobs conducted in the USA, Germany and Russia, have explicitly demonstrated the significant differences in the relative perceptual biases of jobs for students in these countries (Table 4-17, Table 5-1, Table 5-2). The aggregate assessment of the nonmonetary value of the prestigious jobs, PJ, such as CEO, EiC, SM versus GC among different groups of respondents in different countries is shown in Table 5-3.

Table 5-3: The summarized assessment of the nonmonetary value of the prestigious jobs, PJ, such as CEO, EiC, SM versus GC among different groups of respondents in different countries

Relative nonmonetary values of jobs / Categories of respondents	ΔV_{PJ-GC}^{N}
Business students in USA	0.52±0.02
Taxi drivers in USA	0.58±0.02
Construction workers in USA	0.49±0.02
Restaurant waiters in USA	0.55±0.02
Students in Germany	1.2±0.05
Students in Russia	0.62±0.08

Students in Germany are expecting a much higher compensation for the less prestigious job than the students in the USA and Russia. This may reflect the cultural differences in the perception of job in these three culturally and socially different societies.

6 Measuring Nonmonetary Value of Consumer Products

6.1 General Value in Buying Decisions

To find the nonmonetary component of value we used the methodology of indifference point discussed in Chapter 3 (section 3.4). According to the methodology of calculating general value in purchasing decision for consumption products presented in Eq.(3.18) in Chapter 3, the perception of price $U(P)$ contributes to the product general value with the negative sign because the price represents the monetary value that leaves the buyer if the product is purchased, i.e.

$$V^M = -U(P) \tag{6.1}$$

Thus, general values of two products A and B for buying decision can be expressed as

$$\begin{aligned} V_A &= V_A^M + V_A^N = -U(P_A) + V_A^N \\ V_B &= V_B^M + V_B^N = -U(P_B) + V_B^N \end{aligned} \tag{6.2}$$

With the amount of money from the neutral perceptual interval, where the amount is not critically high or low for the buyer, the perception of money can be replaced with the amount as,

$$V_A = V_A^M + V_A^N = -P_A + V_A^N$$
$$V_B = V_B^M + V_B^N = -P_B + V_B^N \qquad (6.3)$$

Thus, the nonmonetary value of the consumer products could be found by the indifference point as

$$\Delta V_{AB}^N = \Delta P_{AB} \qquad (6.4)$$

where A and B are two products to be compared

$$\Delta V_{AB}^N = V_B^N - V_A^N$$
$$\Delta P_{AB} = P_B - P_A \qquad (6.5)$$

Buying decisions are made for the consumption products with the highest general value.

6.2 The Survey Domain and Sampling

6.2.1 The Domain

The surveys on nonmonetary value in buying decisions of consumer products was conducted in Berlin, Germany, in 2016 among university students and in Moscow, Russia, in 2015, 2016 among students of the Moscow Institute of International Affairs (MGIMO). We analyzed and measured the difference of nonmonetary values in buying decision for the following consumer products:

- smartphones,
- cars,
- shoes

6.2.2 Sample Size, Data Verification, and Processing

All incomplete, wrongly or ambiguously filled questionnaires were declared invalid and removed from the survey. The portion of the invalid responses varied from 20% through 40% per each survey. In result, the sample sizes of valid responses for different surveys varied from 130 through 200 valid questionnaires per survey.

All valid responses were collected and statistically processed with the confidence level of 90%.

6.3 Measuring Nonmonetary Values of Smartphones

6.3.1 Measuring the Nonmonetary Value of the *iPhone 6S* versus *NoName* Smartphone in Germany

The participants of this survey (university students in Berlin, Germany) were offered to make a buying decision between an *iPhone 6s* and an unbranded smartphone referred to as *NoName*, which has the same features and technical characteristics as *iPhone 6S* including the screen size, the memory size, processor, the operation system iOS and so on.

The price for the *NoName* smartphone was set to the market average price of €400 (400 euros) for smartphones with similar features and characteristics.

A retailor ReStore is an official *iPhone* distributor for Apple Inc. The price for *iPhone 6S* at ReStore was €650 (650 euros). Thus, to find the indifference point in the buying decision, the price for *iPhone 6S* was varying in the questionnaire as 400, 450, 550, 650, 750, 950, 1150, 1350 и 1500 euros. The last price on the list is more than as twice as higher than the actual price for *iPhone 6S*.

Each respondent had to make a buying decision on *iPhone 6S* vs *NoName* smartphone based on the for each pair of prices according to their own judgement. That pair of prices for which the respondent was indifferent (unsure) what to buy, *iPhone 6S* or *NoName* smartphone, constituted the indifference point for this respondent. The indifference point showed the additional markup price, which the respondent was ready to pay for the *iPhone 6S* versus the *NoName* smartphone. Different respondents might indicate different indifference points.

The total number of participants in this survey was 211, among which 17 filled questionnaires, or 8% of all filled questionnaires, were recognized as invalid and removed from the sample. The number of valid filled questionnaires was 194, which were passed for the processing.

The processed data from the 194 valid questionnaires are presented in Table 6-1 and in Figure 6-1. The middle column "Number of respondents with indifference point" shows the number of the respondents, for whom the respective difference in prices for the *NoName* smartphone (the left column) and for *iPhone 6S* caused the indifference point.

Table 6-1: The survey results on measuring the nonmonetary value of *iPhone 6S* versus a *NoName* smartphone conducted among university students in Germany

Nonmonetary Value of *iPhone 6s* versus a *NoName* smartphone (among German students)				
Price of *NoName* smartphone	Price of *iPhone 6S* smartphone	Number of respondents with indifference point	ΔV_{i6s-NN}^{M}	ΔV_{i6s-NN}^{N}
€400	€400	20	€0	€0
	€550	88	€150	€150
	€750	67	€350	€350
	€950	19	€550	€550
	€1150	0	€750	€750

Number of valid responses:	194	
	Relative nonmonetary values	Relative perceptual bias
Mean on sample:	€243	0.61
Standard deviation:	€153	0.38

Confidence level:	90%	
Confidence interval:	±€18	±0.05
Mean on population:	€243±18	0.61±0.05

The mean nonmonetary value of *iPhone 6S* versus a similar *NoName* smartphone for the students in Germany is €243±18 with the confidence level of 90% (Table 6-1).

Figure 6-1 shows the distribution histogram for the nonmonetary value of *iPhone 6S* versus a similar *NoName* smartphone. This nonmonetary value represents the brand value of *iPhone 6S* for the respondents because there were no other differences of these two smartphones. The dotted line above the distribution histogram in Figure 6-1 shows the associated normal distribution curve.

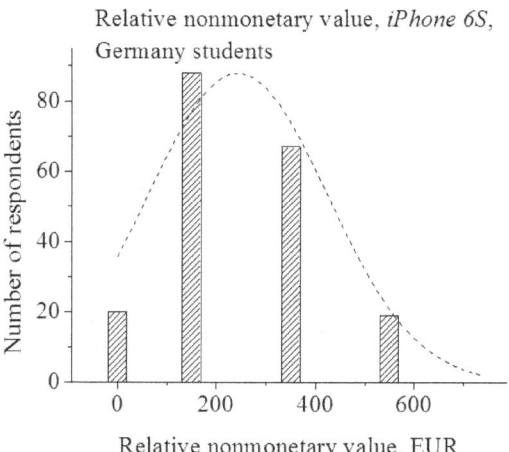

Figure 6-1: The distribution histogram for the nonmonetary value of *iPhone 6S* versus a *NoName* smartphone for university students in Germany. The dashed line indicates the associated normal distribution

6.3.2 Measuring the Nonmonetary Value of the *iPhone 6S* versus *NoName* smartphone in Russia

A similar survey on measuring the nonmonetary value of *iPhone 6S* versus a *NoName* technically matching smartphone was conducted among MGIMO students in Moscow, Russia.

The price for the *NoName* smartphone was set up to 20,000 rubles (₽20 000) and the suggested price for *iPhone 6S* was varying in the survey from 10 to 100 thousand rubles.[9]

---

[9] The exchange rate between US dollar and Russian ruble at the time of the survey was $1 = ₽70.

Table 6-2: The survey results on measuring the nonmonetary value of *iPhone 6S* versus a *NoName* smartphone conducted among university students in Moscow, Russia

Nonmonetary Value of *iPhone 6s* versus a *NoName* smartphone (among Russian students)				
Price of NoName smartphone	Price of iPhone 6S smartphone	Number of respondents with indifference point	ΔV^M_{i6s-NN}	ΔV^N_{i6s-NN}
₽20K	₽20K	6	₽0	-₽0
	₽30K	7	₽10K	₽10K
	₽35K	14	₽15K	₽15K
	₽40K	21	₽20K	₽20K
	₽55K	8	₽35K	₽35K
	₽70K	6	₽50K	₽50K
	₽75K	4	₽55K	₽55K
	₽80K	3	₽60K	₽60K
	₽100K	1	₽80K	₽80K

Number of valid responses:	70	
	Relative nonmonetary values	Relative perceptual bias
Mean on sample:	₽25K	1.26
Standard deviation:	₽18K	0.9

Confidence level:	90%	
Confidence interval:	± ₽3.6K	±0.18
Mean on population:	₽25 ± 3.6K	1.26±0.18

The total number of respondents was 86, but 16 filled questionnaires were disqualified and removed from the sample because they were filled with errors. Thus, the total number of valid questionnaires was 70. The results of this survey are shown in Table 6-2 and Figure 6-2.

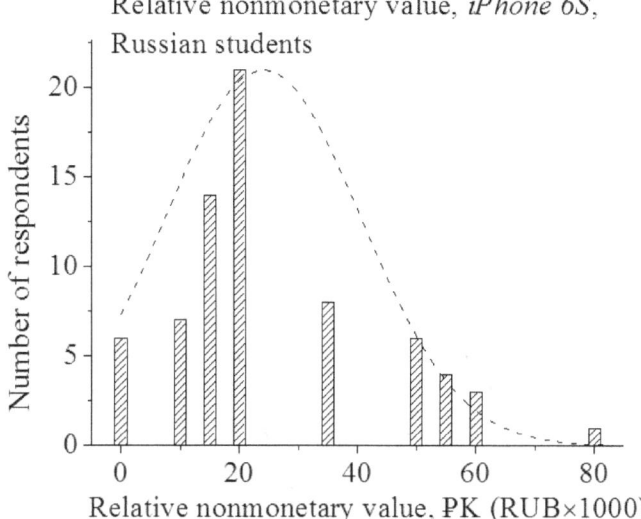

Figure 6-2: The distribution histogram for the nonmonetary value of *iPhone 6S* versus *NoName smartphone* for university students in Russia. The dashed line indicates the associated normal distribution

The dotted line in Figure 6-2 shows the normal distribution on the sample that matches the mean value and the standard deviation presented in Table 6-2.

The results of the surveys on the nonmonetary component of value of *iPhone 6S* versus the *NoName* smartphone conducted in Germany and Russia showed that students were ready to pay extra €243 in Berlin and ₽25K in Moscow for branded iPhone 6S than for the technically the same unbranded smartphone. The nonmonetary bias of the respondents in Berlin was about 61% while in Moscow about 126%. The nonmonetary bias indicated that the respondents in Moscow were more sensitive to the brand name than the respondents in Berlin.

6.4 Measuring the Nonmonetary Value of the *Christian Louboutin* Brand in Russia

The next survey was conducted to measure the nonmonetary value of *Christian Louboutin* brand for ladies' shoes versus similar shoes of a *NoName* brand, i.e. of an unknown manufacturer.

A sample of 52 female respondents was randomly chosen from the university students; 33 completed questionnaires were qualified as valid in the survey. According to the survey logic, the fixed price of ₽5K (5,000 rubles) was set for *NoName* pair of shoes while the price for *Christian Louboutin* shoes was varying from 5 to 80 thousand rubles.[10] The results of this survey are shown in Table 6-3 and Figure 6-3.

Table 6-3: The distribution histogram on measuring the nonmonetary value of *Christian Louboutin* shoe brand conducted among Russian students

Nonmonetary Value of *Christian Louboutin* brand (among Russian students)				
Price of *NoName* shoes	Price of *Christian Louboutin* shoes	Number of respondents with indifference point	ΔV_{CL-NN}^{M}	ΔV_{CL-NN}^{N}
₽5K	₽5K	1	₽0	₽0
	₽10K	10	₽5K	₽5K
	₽20K	14	₽15K	₽15K
	₽50K	7	₽45K	₽45K
	₽80K	1	₽75K	₽75K

Number of valid responses:	33		
		Relative nonmonetary values	Relative perceptual bias
Mean on sample:		₽20K	3.9
Standard deviation:		₽18K	3.6

Confidence level:	90%

---

[10] The exchange rate between US dollar and Russian ruble at the time of the survey was $1 = ₽53.

6 Measuring Nonmonetary Value of Consumer Products

Confidence interval:	± ₽5K	±1.1
Mean on population:	₽20 ±5K	3.9±1.1

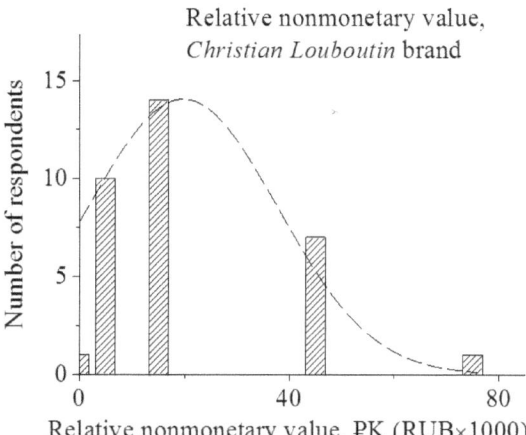

Figure 6-3: The distribution histogram for the nonmonetary value of *Christian Louboutin* shoe brand versus *NoName* shoe manufacturer for university students in Russia. The dashed line indicates the associated normal distribution

The mean value of the nonmonetary value of the *Christian Louboutin* brand was 20 thousand rubles with a quite high standard deviation of 18 thousand rubles. The confidence interval calculated on the sample with 90% confidence level was 15 – 25 thousand rubles (₽15K - ₽25K).

Thus, female students in Moscow have the mean nonmonetary value of the *Christian Louboutin* brand for shoes of about 20 thousand rubles (₽20K). The relative nonmonetary bias of 3.9 shown in Table 6-3 indicates that female students value brand name about four times higher than shoes themselves.

6.5 Measuring the Nonmonetary Value of the *Mazda* Car Brand in Russia

The next survey was dedicated to measuring the nonmonetary value of the *Mazda* car brand. *Mazda 3* model was chosen for the research because this model was very popular among youth in Russia including university students. An imaginary *NoName* car completely matching the body style, all features and characteristics of *Mazda 3* was chosen as the alternative to *Mazda 3*.

In the questionnaire, we priced a *NoName* car as much as 450 thousand rubles (₽450K). The questionnaire suggested the prices for *Mazda 3* in the interval from 450 to 700 thousand rubles ((₽450K - ₽700K).

The initial sample size included 170 students but only 112 completed questionnaires passed the validity check and were used for the further processing and analysis. The results of the survey are shown in Table 6-4 and Figure 6-4.

Table 6-4: Survey results on measuring the nonmonetary value of *Mazda 3* car brand conducted among Russian students

Nonmonetary Value of *Mazda 3* brand (among Russian students)				
Price of a NoName car	Price of Mazda 3 car	Number of respondents at indifference point	ΔV^M_{M3-NN}	ΔV^N_{M3-NN}
₽450K	₽450K	1	₽0	₽0
	₽475K	20	₽25K	₽25K
	₽500K	29	₽50K	₽50K
	₽550K	40	₽100K	₽100K
	₽600K	12	₽150K	₽150K
	₽700K	5	₽250K	₽250K

Number of valid responses:	112		
		Relative nonmonetary values	Relative perceptual bias
Mean on sample:		₽80K	0.18
Standard deviation:		₽56K	0.12

Confidence level:	90%

Confidence interval:	± ₽9K	±0.02
Mean on population:	₽80 ±9K	0.18±0.02

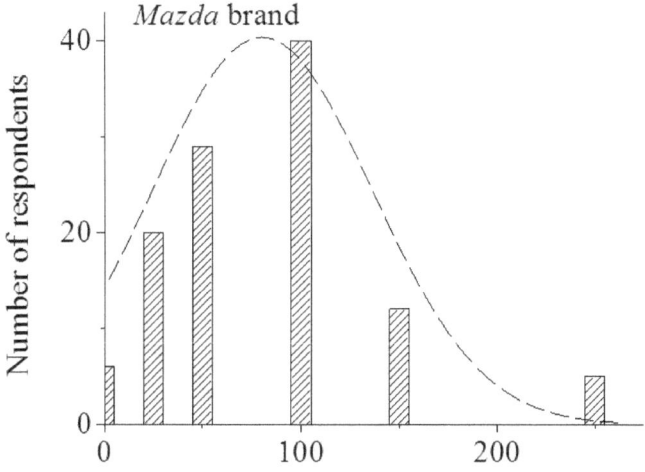

Figure 6-4: The distribution histogram for the nonmonetary value of *Mazda 3* car brand. The dashed line indicates the associated normal distribution

Figure 6-4 shows the distribution histogram for the nonmonetary value for the *Mazda* brand compared to the unbranded car in the perception of the university students. The dotted curve shows the respective normal distribution of the nonmonetary value for the population of university students with 90% confidence level.

As evident from Table 6-4, the mean nonmonetary value of the *Mazda 3* brand was assessed as 80 thousand rubles versus a similar *NoName* car with the standard deviation of 56 thousand rubles. The confidence interval calculated on the sample with 90% confidence was ₽80K ± ₽9K. The relative non-monetary bias for the *Mazda 3* brand is about 18% that represents the perception of the brand name. This indicates that the students in Moscow were not so sensitive to the car brand but mostly value a car as a means of transportation.

7 Measuring Nonmonetary Value of Services

7.1 General Value in Service Purchasing Decisions

Consumers may also have nonmonetary preferences for services based on details, which are not reflected in the monetary components. For example, consumers would prefer to use services where providers are friendlier to their customers.

In this part of our research, we tried to identify the nonmonetary value of branded coffee shops, specialized car services at specialized dealership service centers versus other unbranded car services by finding the indifference points for the respondents similarly to what we did in the surveys related to consumer product purchasing decisions described in the previous chapter.

The monetary value of services are represented by the service price with the negative sign, the same way as it was done for purchasing goods in Chapter 6 and general methodology in Chapter 3. Taking into account that most prices for most common services are priced in the linear perceptual range, the monetary value of services were expressed as negative price as

$$V^M = -P \tag{7.1}$$

Thus, the nonmonetary value of services could be found by the indifference point as

$$\Delta V_{AB}^N = \Delta P_{AB} \tag{7.2}$$

where A and B are two services to be compared

$$\begin{aligned}\Delta V_{AB}^N &= V_B^N - V_A^N \\ \Delta P_{AB} &= P_B - P_A\end{aligned} \tag{7.3}$$

7.2 Measuring the Nonmonetary Value of the *Starbucks* Coffee Brand in Germany

Coffee has become a very popular drink worldwide in the last decades. There are many specialized coffee shops on the market. Many coffee shops offer very similar types of coffee drinks. However, people have preferences to some coffee brands like Starbucks and others. Such preferences could be associated with differences in taste, quality of services, or just related to the familiar brands.

A survey was conducted among university students in Berlin, Germany on measuring the relative nonmonetary value of the *Starbucks* cappuccino versus a *NoName* cappuccino from an unbranded coffee shop. In the survey questionnaire, the respondents should choose a cup of *NoName* cappuccino or a cup of cappuccino from *Starbucks* depending on the prices or indicate the indifference in the choice. The price for a cup of cappuccino from an unbranded coffee shop, which is referred to as *NoName*, was set to €2 (2 euro) while the price for a cup of *Starbucks* cappuccino was varying from €0.5 through €20 per cup to find the indifference point.

Totally, 210 university students from Berlin, Germany, participated in the survey, but 22 or 11% of all filled questionnaires were disqualified due to respondents' errors. Thus, totally 188 responses were qualified as valid for the processing.

We used the same logic for finding the nonmonetary value of *Starbucks* brand cappuccino versus a *NoName* cappuccino as we did for finding the nonmonetary value for goods in Chapter 6.

The results of the survey are shown in Table 7-1 and Figure 7-1.

Table 7-1: The survey results on measuring the nonmonetary value of coffee from *Starbucks* versus a coffee from *NoName* conducted among German students

Nonmonetary Value of *Starbucks* brand (among German students)				
Price of *NoName* coffee	Price of *Starbucks* coffee	Number of respondents with indifference point	ΔV^M_{Sb-NN}	ΔV^N_{Sb-NN}
€2	€3	6	€1	€1
	€5	59	€3	€3
	€8	71	€6	€6
	€11	49	€9	€9
	€13	3	€11	€11

Number of valid responses:	188	
	Relative nonmonetary values	Relative perceptual bias
Mean on sample:	€5.8	2.9
Standard deviation:	€2.5	1.3

Confidence level:	90%	
Confidence interval:	± €0.3	±0.15
Mean on population:	€5.8 ±0.3	2.9±0.15

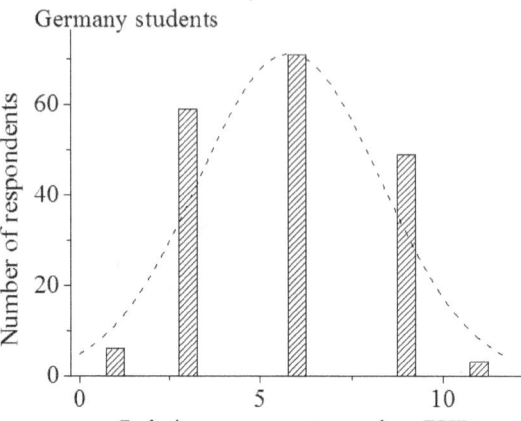

Figure 7-1: The distribution histogram for the nonmonetary value of *Starbucks* coffee versus *NoName* coffee among university students in Berlin, Germany. The dashed curve indicates the associated normal distribution

The mean nonmonetary value of *Starbucks* coffee for German students versus a *NoName* coffee presented in Table 7-1 indicate that student are ready to pay on average €5.8 or 180% more for the *Starbucks* cappuccino than for the *NoName* cappuccino.

It is interesting to note that in case of Starbuck, the sentiments towards *Starbuck* brand versus other coffee brands are stronger in Germany than in Russia, which is quite opposite to the sentiments towards *iPhone* versus no brand mobile phones.

It looks that Germans are ready to pay more for their favorite brands than Russians, if the price (monetary value) is reasonably low. On the other hand, Russians show the greater sentiments and ready to pay extra price than Germans for the expensive brands. Such a apparently controversial sentimental behavior is aligned with the consumer behavior described in behavioral economics (Kahneman, Slovic, & Tversky, 1982; Kahneman & Tversky, 2000; Kahneman, 2011).

7.3 Measuring the Nonmonetary Value of Specialized Car Services in Russia

In the survey dedicated to car services in Russia, the questionnaire offered the choice between a *NoName* private garage service versus service at a service center at a specialized dealership at a premium price relative to the *NoName* garage service. The price for the service at a *NoName* garage was set to 7 thousand rubles and a list of the suggested prices for the same service at a specialized dealership was set to 7, 8, 10, 12, 15, and 20 thousand Russian rubles (₽). The nonmonetary value of the service at a specialized dealership was calculated by the difference of prices at the indifference point according to Eq.(6.4).

The total number of respondents (university students in Moscow, Russia) in this survey was 169 but the number of valid responses was 100. The other returned questionnaires were disqualified and discarded as invalid due to their incompleteness or inaccuracies, which could lead to ambiguities. The summary of the nonmonetary values of the specialized car services versus a *NoName* service is shown in Table 7-2 and Figure 7-2.

Table 7-2: Survey results on measuring nonmonetary value of car service at a specialized center versus service at *NoName* garage conducted among Russian students

Nonmonetary Value of car service at a specialized center (among Russian students)				
Price of NoName car service	Price of specialized center car service	Number of respondents at the indifference point	ΔV^M_{M3-NN}	ΔV^N_{M3-NN}
₽7K	₽7K	4	₽0	₽0
	₽8K	24	₽1K	₽1K
	₽10K	27	₽3K	₽3K
	₽12K	24	₽5K	₽5K
	₽15K	16	₽8K	₽8K
	₽20K	5	₽13K	₽13K

Number of valid responses:	100

	Relative nonmonetary values	Relative perceptual bias
Mean on sample:	₽4.2K	0.6
Standard deviation:	₽3.2K	0.45

Confidence level:	90%	
Confidence interval:	± ₽0.5K	±0.07
Mean on population:	₽4.2 ±0.5K	0.6±0.07

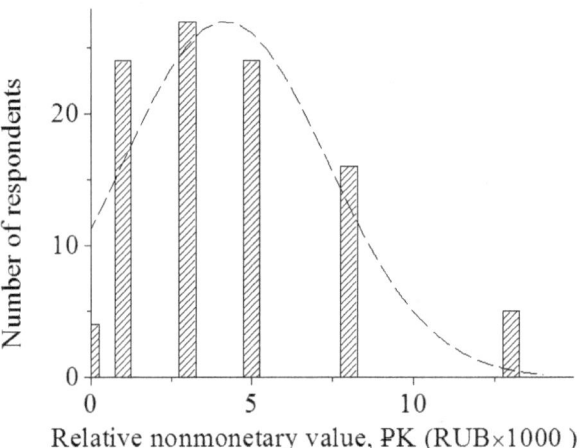

Figure 7-2: The distribution diagram for the nonmonetary value of car service at a Specialized Center. The dashed line indicates the associated normal distribution

The survey has clearly demonstrated that the respondents are ready pay 4,200 ruble more at the specialized car services at dealerships rather than at the *NoName* garages. That makes the relative nonmonetary bias equal 60%.

7.4 Measuring the Nonmetary Value of Airlines in Russia

Many airlines operate throughout the world and offer a diversity of fares and levels of services. Some passengers prefer to go with the cheapest airlines while other passengers prefer quality of services over the price. In this part of our research, the goal was to measure the nonmonetary value of airlines in the perception of passengers. We compared two Russian airlines: the Russian major airline *Aeroflot*[11] with a small airline *KavMinVodyAvia*[12]. Both carriers fly on the rout Moscow-Sochi and offer the same level of service that includes one piece of checked-in baggage up to 20 kg per passenger and meal. Thus, the only difference between these two carriers on the route Moscow-Sochi is the airline's brand name and prestige, i.e. the nonmonetary value of the airline in the perception of passengers. To calculate the difference of the nonmonetary values of these two airlines, we have to identify the indifference points in the perception of the passengers, i.e. how much passengers are ready to pay extra to fly with *Aeroflot* rather than with *KavMinVodyAvia*.

In the survey questionnaire, we used a fixed fare of 11 thousand rubles for one roundtrip ticket Moscow-Sochi on *KavMinVodyAvia*. The airfare for a similar flight with Aeroflot was varying from 11 to 25 thousand rubles.

The total number of Moscow students participating in this survey was 160, however only 138 completed questionnaires were qualified as valid. The numbers of respondents by their indifferent points and the appropriate nonmonetary values along with the number of respondents are shown in Table 7-3 and Figure 7-3.

---

[11] *Аэрофлот* (in Russian)

[12] *КавМинВодыАвиа* (in Russian)

Table 7-3: The survey results on nonmonetary value of a round-trip flight with Aeroflot (Af) versus a similar flight with *KavMinVodyAvia* (KMV) conducted among Russian students

Nonmonetary Value of a round-trip flight with Aeroflot versus a similar flight with *KavMinVodyAvia* (among Russian students)				
Price of a roundtrip ticket on *KavMinVodyAvia*	Price of a roundtrip ticket on Aeroflot	Number of respondents at the indifference point	ΔV^M_{Af-KMV}	ΔV^N_{Af-KMV}
₽11K	₽11K	11	₽0	₽0
	₽13K	31	₽2K	₽2K
	₽15K	32	₽4K	₽4K
	₽18K	45	₽7K	₽7K
	₽21K	19	₽10K	₽10K
	₽25K	0	₽14K	₽14K

Number of valid responses:	138	
	Relative nonmonetary values	Relative perceptual bias
Mean on sample:	₽5.0K	0.46
Standard deviation:	₽3.0K	0.27

Confidence level:	90%	
Confidence interval:	± ₽0.4K	±0.04
Mean on population:	₽5.0 ±0.4K	0.46±0.04

7 Measuring Nonmonetary Value of Services

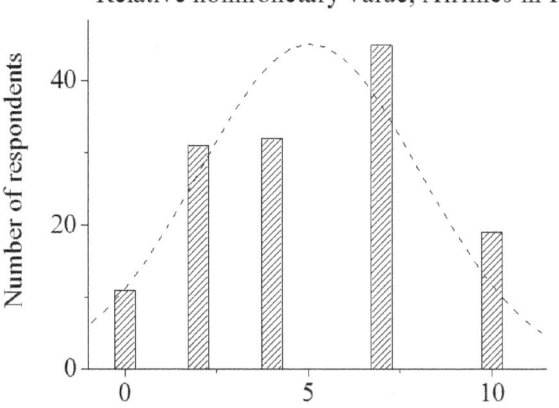

Figure 7-3: The distribution histogram for the nonmonetary value of a round-trip flight with *Aeroflot* versus a similar flight with *KavMinVodyAvia*. The dashed line indicates the associated normal distribution

Table 7-3 shows the statistical results of the survey. The mean nonmonetary value of a round-trip flight with *Aeroflot* versus a similar flight with *KavMinVodyAvia* was 5.0 thousand rubles, the standard deviation was 3.0 thousand rubles, and confidence interval was 4.6 – 5.5 thousand rubles calculated with 90% confidence level. The survey results presented in Table 7-3 indicate that the nonmonetary bias of Aeroflot is 46%, i.e. the respondents value Aeroflot more than just a carrier that can bring them from one city to another with the same quality of services.

8 Transaction Power and Efficiency

8.1 Increasing General Value

Any decision tend to increase general value. The participants of any free will transaction or action have the objective of increasing their general value. Each participant makes a decision to pursue with a transaction or an action, if the resultant general value (after the transaction or action) for this participant is expected to increase relative to the initial general value (before the transaction or action), This, the increment of the general value shiouks be positive for each participant k,

$$\Delta V_k = V_k^{after} - V_k^{before} > 0 \qquad (8.1)$$

The difference between general values after and before the action or transaction ΔV_k is referred to as the added general value for the action or transaction undertaken by the participant. This principle can be paraphrased as follows:
- Any decision leads to an increase of general value
- The added general value should increase for each participant in result of any action or transaction

> Any decision leads to an increase of general value.

> The added general value should increase for each participant in result of any action or transaction

A simple illustration of this concept can be given with the transaction of purchasing a loaf of bread by a consumer from a baker. The baker makes the bread for profit and has zero nonmonetary value for the produced bread.[13] Thus, the increment of general value for the baker from this transaction is the generated profit, which is

$$\Delta V_{Baker} = V_{Baker}^{after} - V_{Baker}^{before} = P - C > 0 \qquad (8.2)$$

where P is the sales price and C is the total costs associated with the production and sale of a loaf of bread. The increment of general value for the consumer is

$$\Delta V_{Consumer} = V_{Consumer}^{after} - V_{Consumer}^{before} = V_{Consumer}^{N} - P > 0 \qquad (8.3)$$

where $V_{Consumer}^{N}$ reperesents the consumer's satisfaction from consuming the bread.

A good illustration of this principle can be given with trade of post stamps by two collectors 1 and 2. Collector 1 A has a poststamp A of market value of $P_A = \$1.00$ and collector 2 B has a poststamp B of nominal value of $P_B = \$0.25$. Assume $P_A > P_B$. Collector 1 trades his poststamp A for poststamp B and pays extra $\$5.00$ to collector 2 for the trade. Such a trade results in the increase of general value for both collectors as

---

[13] For simplicity, we ignore such sentimental factors as the baker's pride about the job and the produced products.

$$\begin{aligned}
\Delta V_1 &= V_1^{After} - V_1^{Before} = \Delta V_A^M + \Delta V_A^N = \\
&= \$0.25 - \$1.00 - \$5.00 + V_1^{NB} - V_1^{NA} = \\
&= -\$5.75 + V_1^{NB} - V_1^{NA} > 0 \\
\Delta V_2 &= V_2^{After} - V_2^{Before} = \Delta V_2^M + \Delta V_2^N = \\
&= \$5.00 + \$1.00 - \$0.25 + V_2^{NA} - V_2^{NB} = \\
&= \$5.75 + V_2^{NA} - V_2^{NB} > 0
\end{aligned} \quad (8.4)$$

where V_1^{NA} and V_1^{NB} are the nonmonetary values of poststamps A and B in the perception of collector 1, and V_2^{NA} and V_2^{NB} are the nonmonetary values of poststamps A and B in the perception of collector 2.

8.2 Transaction Power and Efficiency

8.2.1 Transaction Power

Any transaction or action should increase general values for all involved parties or at least does not reduce them. Let's consider a transaction between two participants and introduce the term ***transaction power*** which we define as the total added general value for all participants of the transaction, i.e.

$$W = \Delta V_1 + \Delta V_2 \quad (8.5)$$

where W is the transaction power and ΔV_1 and ΔV_2 are the added general values for participants 1 and 2 in the transaction. It is obvious from the principle of increasing general value in Eq.(8.1) that all added general values must be positive, i.e.

$$\Delta V_1 > 0, \quad \Delta V_2 > 0 \quad (8.6)$$

and hence, the transaction power in Eq.(8.5) is positive too

$$\Delta W > 0 \quad (8.7)$$

8.2.2 Transaction Efficiency

Different participants may receive different added general values from the transaction. A ***fair transaction*** is understood as a transaction where both participants get the same added general value, i.e.

$$\Delta V_1 = \Delta V_2 \qquad (8.8)$$

On the other hand, we consider a transaction unfair, if the added general value for one participant in much higher than the added general value for another participant. The less difference between the added general values of the transaction for both participants, the more fair the transaction.

Let's introduce the term ***transaction efficiency***, which reflects a degree of fairness of a transaction. The transaction efficiency is measured in terms of closeness of the added general values for both participants as

$$E = 4\frac{\Delta V_1 \Delta V_2}{(\Delta V_1 + \Delta V_2)^2} = 4\frac{\Delta V_1 \Delta V_2}{W^2} \qquad (8.9)$$

where E is the transaction efficiency.

According to the definition in Eq. (8.9), transaction efficiency is a parameter in the range between zero and one, i.e. $E \in [0,1]$. If both participants of a transaction receive equal added general values as in Eq.(8,8), then, according to Eq.(8.9) $E = 1$ and the transaction is referred to as ***perfectly efficient***, i.e. the transaction is considered the most fair. On the other hand, in the extreme case, when one participant receives very little added general value relative to the added general value received by another participant, i.e. $\Delta V_1 \ll \Delta V_2$ or $\Delta V_2 \ll \Delta V_1$, then the transaction is considered ***extremely inefficient*** and its efficiency tends to zero, $E \to 0$, i.e., the transaction is considered extremely unfair.

Please note that transaction efficiency does not depend on the transaction power

$$E = 4\frac{\Delta V_1(W - \Delta V_1)}{W} = 4\frac{\Delta V_2(W - \Delta V_2)}{W} \qquad (8.10)$$

A transaction can be of any degree of its efficiency with any transaction power, high or low.

8.3 Relative Addedd General Value

Let's call the ratio of the added general value for participant k over the total transaction power the **relative added general value** for participant k, α_1, i.e.

$$\alpha_k = \frac{\Delta V_k}{W} \tag{8.11}$$

and according to Eqs.(8.5), (8.6) and (8,11)

$$0 < \alpha_k < 1 \tag{8.12}$$

If there are only two participants in the transaction, then

$$\alpha_1 + \alpha_2 = 1 \tag{8.13}$$

Then by the definition of transaction efficiency given in Eq. (8.9), the transaction efficiency can be rewritten as

$$E = 4\alpha_1 \alpha_2 \tag{8.14}$$

and hence,

$$E = 4\alpha_1(1-\alpha_1) \quad \text{or} \quad E = 4\alpha_2(1-\alpha_2) \tag{8.15}$$

If $\alpha_1 = \alpha_2 = \frac{1}{2}$, then the transaction is perfectly efficient, i.e., $E = 1$. On the other hand, if $\alpha_1 \ll 0$ or $\alpha_2 \ll 0$, then $E \to 0$ and the transaction is extremely inefficient as shown in Figure 8-1.

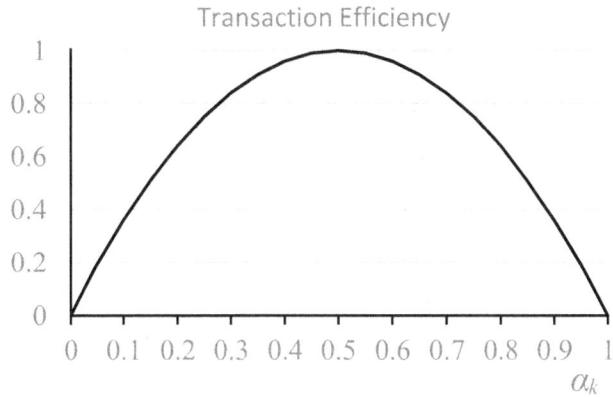

Figure 8-1: Transaction efficiency as function of the relative added general value α_k of one of the participants

As is evident from Figure 8-1, the transaction between two participants is perfectly efficient when the relative added general values for both participants, α_1 and α_2, equal one half of the total transaction power, W.

8.4 Efficiency of Purely Monetary Transactions

A good example of purely monetary transactions could be given in supply chain. Suppose a wholesales reseller 1 sells a certain product A to another reseller 2 at price P per unit. Reseller 1 purchased the product at price P_1 per unit. Reseller 2 resells the product at price P_2 per unit. Assume $P_2 > P > P_1$. Both resellers have no nonmonetary component of value for the product and are interested in the monetary profit only. For simplicity, we are ignoring all transaction costs. Thus this transaction is purely monetary.

The added general value for this transaction includes only monetary components of value, i.e.

$$\Delta V_1 = P - P_1 \quad \text{and} \quad \Delta V_2 = P_2 - P \tag{8.16}$$

According to Eq.(8.5), the transaction power for this transaction is

$$W = \Delta V_1 + \Delta V_2 = P_2 - P_1 \tag{8.17}$$

and the the transaction efficiency is

$$E = 4 \frac{\Delta V_1 \Delta V_2}{\left(\Delta V_1 + \Delta V_2\right)^2} = 4 \frac{(P - P_1)(P_2 - P)}{\left(P_2 - P_1\right)^2} \tag{8.18}$$

The relative added general value for this transaction is

$$\alpha_1 = \frac{\Delta V_1}{W} = \frac{P - P_1}{P_2 - P_1} \quad \text{and} \quad \alpha_2 = \frac{\Delta V_2}{W} = \frac{P_2 - P}{P_2 - P_1} \tag{8.19}$$

If the transaction is fair, i.e. $P = (P_2 - P_1)/2$, then the the transaction is efficient with the efficiency $E = 1$ and the relative added general value for both resellers are $\alpha_1 = \alpha_2 = \frac{1}{2}$.

On the other hand, if the resellers obrain different added values this transaction, for instance, $\Delta V_1 = 1/3 \Delta V_2$, then relative added values $\alpha_1 = 1/4$ and $\alpha_2 = 3/4$. This transaction is not fair and according to Eq.(8.14), its efficiency $E = 4*1/4*3/4 = \frac{3}{4}$.

8.5 Efficiency of Purely Nonmonetary Transactions

Suppose two individuals, 1 and 2, are walking on a beach. Individual 1 found a nice shell and individual 2 found a nice rock. Both the rock and the shell do not have market values, hence their monetary values equal zero. However, individual 1 likes the rock better than the shell and individual 2 likes the shell better than the rock. It means that

$$V_1^{NR} > V_1^{NS} \quad \text{and} \quad V_2^{NS} > V_2^{NR} \qquad (8.20)$$

and V_1^{NR} and V_1^{NS} are the nonmonetary values of the rock and of the shell, respectively, in the perception of individual 1. Similarly, V_2^{NR} and V_2^{NS} are the nonmonetary values of the rock and of the shell, respectively, in the perception of individual 2.

The individuals decided to trade the rock and the shell without any monetary compensation. The added general values for individual 1 ans 2 in this trade were

$$\Delta V_1 = V_1^{NR} - V_1^{NS} > 0 \quad \text{and} \quad \Delta V_2 = V_2^{NS} - V_2^{NR} > 0 \qquad (8.21)$$

and hence, the transaction power was

$$W = \Delta V_1 + \Delta V_2 = V_1^{NR} - V_1^{NS} + V_2^{NS} - V_2^{NR} \qquad (8.22)$$

The relative added general values for individuals 1 and 2 in this trade were

$$\alpha_1 = \frac{\Delta V_1}{W} = \frac{V_1^{NR} - V_1^{NS}}{V_1^{NR} - V_1^{NS} + V_2^{NS} - V_2^{NR}}$$

$$\alpha_B = \frac{\Delta V_2}{W} = \frac{V_2^{NS} - V_2^{NR}}{V_1^{NR} - V_1^{NS} + V_2^{NS} - V_2^{NR}} \qquad (8.23)$$

and the transaction efficiency was

$$E = 4\frac{\Delta V_1 \Delta V_2}{\left(\Delta V_1 + \Delta V_2\right)^2} = 4\frac{(V_1^{NR} - V_1^{NS})(V_2^{NS} - V_2^{NR})}{\left(V_1^{NR} - V_1^{NS} + V_2^{NS} - V_2^{NR}\right)^2} \qquad (8.24)$$

The transaction efficiency in this trade is maximum when both individuals obtain equal nonmonetary added general value, i.e.

$$\Delta V_1 = \Delta V_2 \quad \text{or} \quad V_1^{NR} - V_2^{NS} = V_2^{NS} - V_2^{NR} \qquad (8.25)$$

8.6 Efficiency of Transactions with Mixed Components

Suppose art collector 1 has picture A of market value P_A and art collector 2 has picture B of market value P_B. These art collectors decide to trade their pictures. Art collector 2 pays P_0 to art collector 1 to close the trade. Please keep in mind that those art collectors are not art traders and have their collections to enjoy them, thus the nonmonetary component of value plays a significant role in their decision making.

Let's analyze the former mentioned picture trade from the general value perspective. Picture A has monetary market value P_A and nonmonetary value V_1^{NA} in the perception of art collector 1. Picture B has monetary market value P_B and nonmonetary value V_2^{NB} in the perception of art collector 2. Picture A in the perception of art collector 2 has nonmonetary value V_2^{NA} and picture B in the perception of art collector 1 has nonmonetary value V_1^{NB}.

The added general value for each art collector in this trade will be

$$\begin{aligned}
\Delta V_1 &= P_B + P_0 + V_1^{NB} - P_A - V_1^{NA} = \\
&= \Delta P_{AB0} + \Delta V_1^{NAB} > 0 \\
\Delta V_2 &= P_A + V_2^{NA} - P_B - P_0 - V_2^{NB} \\
&= -\Delta P_{AB0} + \Delta V_2^{NBA} > 0
\end{aligned} \qquad (8.26)$$

where

$$\begin{aligned}
\Delta P_{AB0} &= P_B + P_0 - P_A \\
\Delta V_1^{NAB} &= V_1^{NB} - V_1^{NA} \\
\Delta V_2^{NBA} &= V_2^{NA} - V_2^{NB}
\end{aligned} \qquad (8.27)$$

ΔP_{AB0} is the difference og the monetary values of pictures A and B including the additional payment P_0. ΔV_1^{NAB} is the added nonmonetary value for art collector 1, i.e. the difference of nonmonetary values of pictures B and A in the perception of art collector 1 while ΔV_2^{NBA} is the added nonmonetary value for art collector 2, i.e. the difference of nonmonetary values of pictures A and B in the perception of art collector 2.

The transaction power according to Eq.(8.5) is

$$W = \Delta V_A + \Delta V_B = \\ = V_1^{NB} - V_1^{NA} + V_2^{NA} - V_2^{NB} = \\ = \Delta V_1^{NAB} + \Delta V_2^{NBA} = \\ = \Delta V_{12}^{NA} - \Delta V_{12}^{NB} \qquad (8.28)$$

where ΔV_{12}^{NA} and ΔV_{12}^{NB} are the differences in nonmonetary values of pictures A and B in the perception of art collectors 1 and 2 as

$$\Delta V_{12}^{NA} = V_2^{NA} - V_1^{NA} \\ \Delta V_{12}^{NB} = V_2^{NB} - V_1^{NB} \qquad (8.29)$$

As evident from Eqs.(8.28) and (8.29), the transaction power for the picture trade does not depend on the monetary components of the values, P_A, P_B, and P_0, and represents the difference of nonmonetary) values of the pictures in perception of the art collectors. The monetary component of values does not play a role in the transaction power because the market values of the pictured did not change in the result of the trade.

The relative added general values for art collectors 1 and 2 in this trade is

$$\alpha_1 = \frac{\Delta V_1}{W} = \frac{\Delta P_{AB0} + \Delta V_1^{NAB}}{\Delta V_1^{NAB} + \Delta V_2^{NBA}} = \frac{\Delta P_{AB0} + \Delta V_1^{NAB}}{\Delta V_{12}^{NA} - \Delta V_{12}^{NB}} \\ \alpha_2 = \frac{\Delta V_2}{W} = \frac{-\Delta P_{AB0} + \Delta V_2^{NBA}}{\Delta V_1^{NAB} + \Delta V_2^{NBA}} = \frac{-\Delta P_{AB0} + \Delta V_2^{NBA}}{\Delta V_{12}^{NA} - \Delta V_{12}^{NB}} \qquad (8.30)$$

and the transaction efficiency is

$$E = 4\frac{\Delta V_1 \Delta V_2}{(\Delta V_1 + \Delta V_2)^2} =$$

$$= 4\frac{(\Delta P_{AB0} + \Delta V_1^{NAB})(-\Delta P_{AB0} + \Delta V_2^{NBA})}{(\Delta V_1^{NAB} + \Delta V_2^{NBA})^2} = \quad (8.31)$$

$$= 4\frac{(\Delta P_{AB0} + \Delta V_1^{NAB})(-\Delta P_{AB0} + \Delta V_2^{NBA})}{(\Delta V_{12}^{NA} - \Delta V_{12}^{NB})^2}$$

According to the condition in Eq.(8.8), the transaction is fair if $\Delta V_1 = \Delta V_2$, i.e.

$$\Delta P_{AB0} + \Delta V_1^{NAB} = -\Delta P_{AB0} + \Delta V_2^{NBA} \quad (8.32)$$

that can be rewritten as

$$P_B + P_0 - P_A = \frac{1}{2}(\Delta V_2^{NBA} - \Delta V_1^{NAB}) =$$

$$= \frac{1}{2}(V_2^{NA} - V_2^{NB} - V_1^{NB} + V_1^{NA}) \quad (8.33)$$

Thus, the fair amount P_0, which art collector 2 paid to art collector 1 can be found from Eq.(8.33) as

$$P_0 = P_A - P_B + \frac{1}{2}(\Delta V_2^{NBA} - \Delta V_1^{NAB}) =$$

$$= P_A - P_B + \frac{1}{2}(V_2^{NA} - V_2^{NB} - V_1^{NB} + V_1^{NA}) \quad (8.34)$$

which is equal to the difference between the monetary values of the pictures adjusted by the differences in nonmonetary values of the pictures in the perception of art collectors 1 and 2.

8.7 Circulation of General Values versus Economic Factors

Circulation of money against economic factors such as labor, goods, and services is a driving force of a market economy. This is one of the fundamental principles of market economy. A simplified version of such a circulation is shown in Figure 8-2. Individuals offer their labor to firms through the factor markets and receive monetary compensation as illustrated in the bottom part of the figure. Firms use the labor to produce goods or render services and offer them to the product markets for money. Individuals buy the goods and services from the product markets paying with the money received as the compensation for their labor as illustrated in the upper part of the figure.

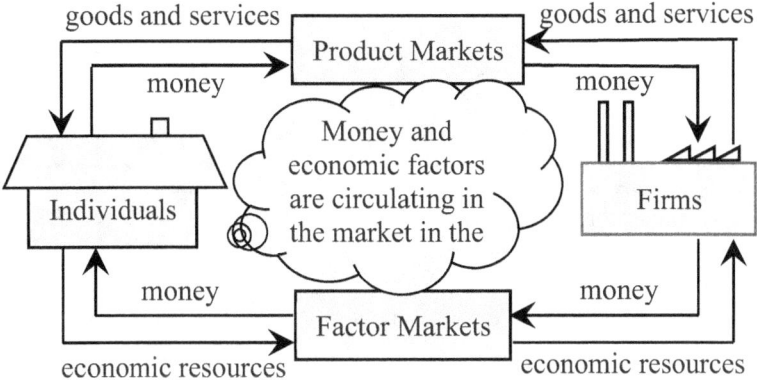

Figure 8-2: Traditional view on circulation of money versus economic factors and products in the market economy

The commonly accepted principle of circulation of money against circulation of factors presumes money to be the only compensation for the labor and ignores workers' satisfaction with the job, location, convenience, work environment and many other factors making individuals satisfied with their job.

Nonmonetary factors influencing individuals in their choice of jobs have been discussed in Chapter 2, and the methodology of measuring the nonmonetary values of such factors were discussed in Chapters 3 and 4. It is clear that nonmonetary factors are adding to the monetary compensation of employees for offering their labor to firms. The combination of monetary and nonmonetary compensations of employees constitutes general value for the employees received form the firms for their labor. Thus, the traditional principle of the circulation of money against products and services in the products markets shown in Figure 8-2 can be extended as circulation of general value against products and services in the products markets as illustrated in Figure 8-3.

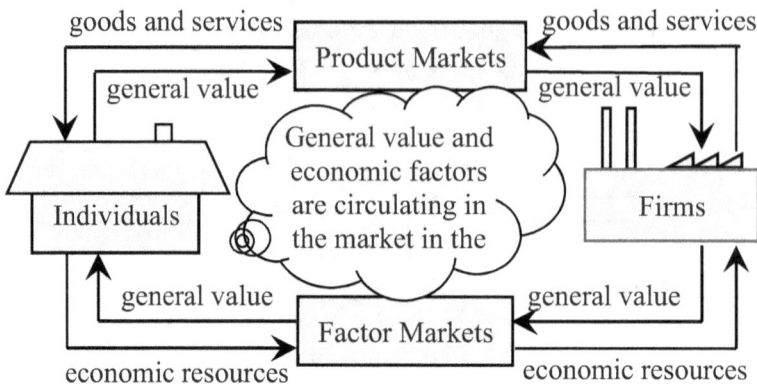

Figure 8-3: Circulation of general value versus economic factors and products in the market economy

Individuals can offer their labor for the compensation that consists of money and nonmonetary compensation as described above. As an extreme case, individuals can do the work as charity or just for the satisfaction the job bring to them. Such an approach provides the more comprehensive and generalized principle of the circulation of factors against product and services in the economy. Such a generalized principle better describes market economy as well as other other forms of economies in the real world.

9 Trading a Paper Clip for a Single Family Home

9.1 From a Paper Clip to a Single Family House

You may have heard an exciting story about an individual, who started with a paper clip and, through a chain of barter trades without additional payments, has turned it into a single-family house. According to the publication[14], Kyle MacDonald from Canada has traded a big red clip into a house in fourteen barter trades. That person started with a paper clip, then traded it for a pen, then traded the pen for a lighter, and so on ... ending up with a single-family house without a single penny of additional payments in this chain of exchanges. The story is nice, but there is a question, whether it is possible from the economic standpoint. Every exchange is based on matching the values of the exchanged

---

[14] From paper-clip to house in 14 trades (July 7, 2006). CBC News, https://www.cbc.ca/news/canada/from-paper-clip-to-house-in-14-trades-1.573973

Man Turns Paper Clip into House (July 11, 2006), BBC News, http://news.bbc.co.uk/2/hi/technology/5167388.stm

items. Thus, how is it possible to advance from a very cheap paper clip to a quite expensive single-family house? How did the trader managed keep permanently increasing value in the chain of barter exchanges? (Aityan, 2020b)

9.2   A Barter Chain Trader versus a Consumer

A consumer makes a purchase or trade decision by considering general value of the product including both, monetary and nonmonetary values, because the consumer has the need and intention of using the product obtained in the trade. On the other hand, a barter chain trader has no intention of using the product but keeps the chain of trades to grow his own monetary value. Making trading decisions, the barter chain trader ignores the nonmonetary value of the traded products. The trader may deal with different consumers in each trade.

Thus, the difference between a trader and a consumer is that the trader has no intention of using the product, but only wants to trade it for a higher monetary value, while the consumer has a need for the product. This difference can be expressed in terms of the nonmonetary values of the same product for the trader and for the consumer. For the trader, the nonmonetary value of the product is zero, while for the consumer, the nonmonetary value should be positive because of the need in the product.

Suppose the trader is in possession of product A and the consumer is in possession of product B. Let's analyze the consumer and the trader view on the potential barter trade, i.e. exchange of these products without additional payment. General values of products A and B in the perception of the trader are denoted as VT_A and VT_B, respectively, while in the perception of the consumer they as VC_A and VC_B. The monetary and nonmonetary values of these products in the perception of the trader are VT_A^M, VT_A^N and VT_B^M, VT_B^N, respectively. As soon as the trader is not interested in using these products, but just in their monetary values only, the nonmonetary value of these products in the trader's perception are equal to zero,

$$VT_A^N = VT_B^N = 0 \qquad (9.1)$$

and hence, the general values of these products in the perception of the trader are equal to their monetary values as

$$VT_A = VT_A^M \quad \text{and} \quad VT_B = VT_B^M \tag{9.2}$$

On the other hand, the general values of these products in the perception of the consumer are

$$VC_A = VC_A^M + VC_A^N \quad \text{and} \quad VC_B = VC_B^M + VC_B^N \tag{9.3}$$

where VC_A^M, VC_A^N and VC_B^M, VC_B^N are monetary and nonmonetary values of products A and B in the consumer's perception, respectively. Note that the consumer is interested in both, monetary and nonmonetary values of the products.

Figure 9-1 shows all possible combinations of monetary and nonmonetary values of products A and B in the perception of the trader and the consumer that would or would not lead to a barter trade (an exchange without payment from any side) of these products between the trader and the consumer.

It is reasonable to assume that the monetary values for each product are the same for the trader and for the consumer, which are the market values of the products, i.e.

$$VT_A^M = VC_A^M \quad \text{and} \quad VT_B^M = VC_B^M \tag{9.4}$$

however, this assumption is not crucial for the analysis.

To perform a trade, the trader should agree to trade product A for product B with the consumer and the consumer should agree to trade product B for product A with the trader.

In the situation shown in Figure 9-1(a), the general value of product B (offered by the consumer) to the trader is lower than the general value of product A (in possession of the trader) and for this reason the trader is not willing to trade his product A for product B. From the consumer's view, the general value of product A offered by the trader is lower than the general value of product B offered by the consumer and the consumer also does not want such a trade. There is no trade in this case. Note, that the barter chain trader considers only monetary value of both products, because he has no intention of using either product and is interested in them only as the objects for trading to increase his monetary value.

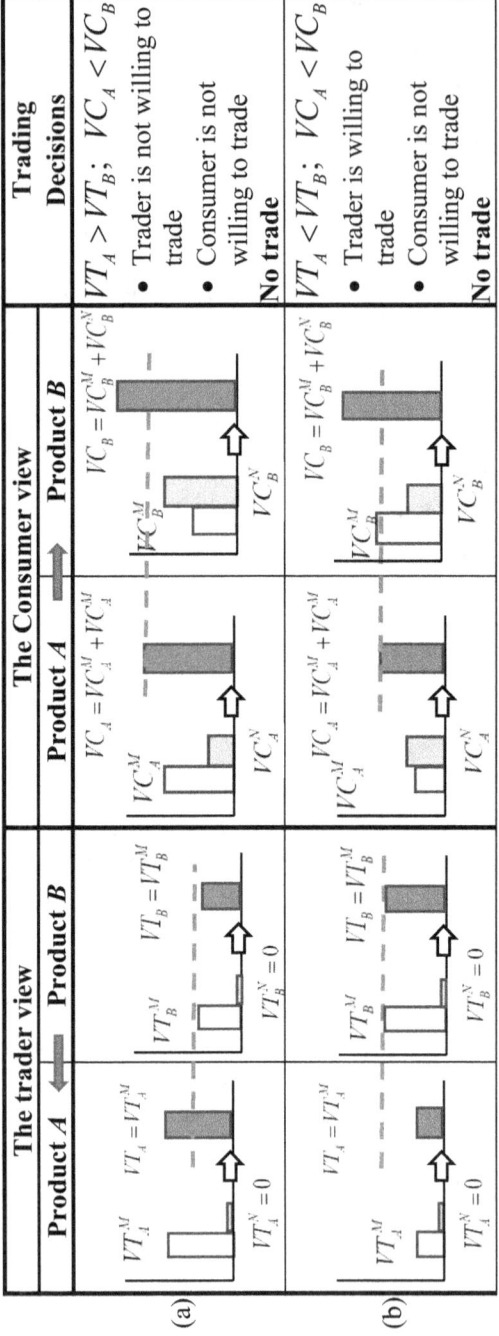

Figure 9-1(a,b): The trader and the consumer views on the general value of the barter trade and their trading decisions. In (a), (b), and (c) at least one party is not interested in the trade. In (d) both parties are interested in the trade and the trade takes place.

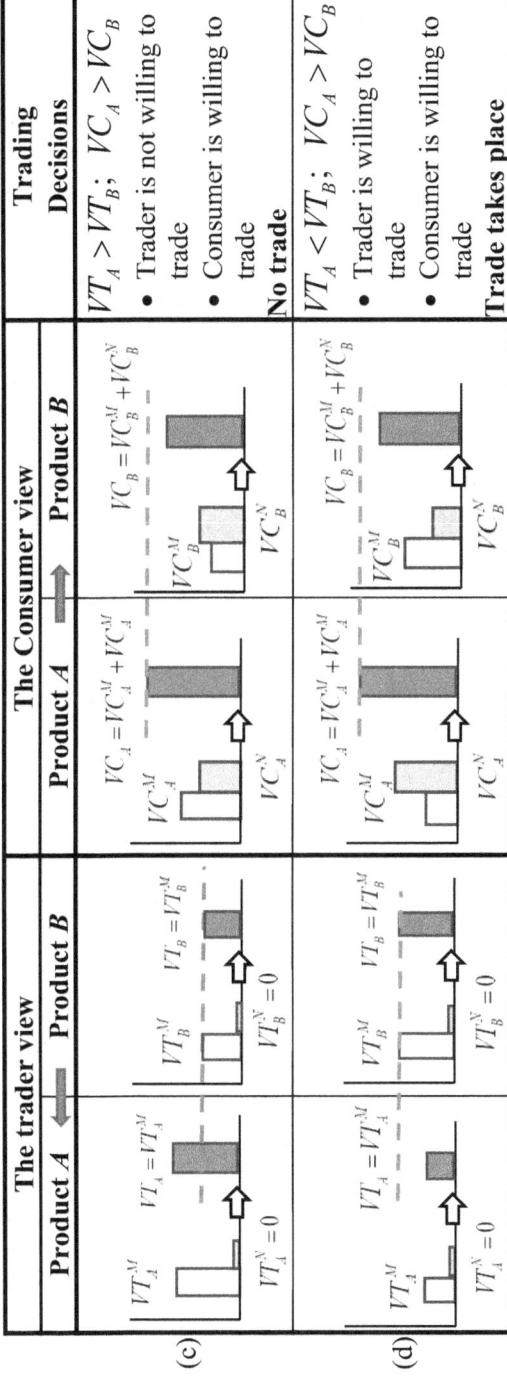

Figure 9-1 (c,d): The trader and the consumer views on the general value of the barter trade and their trading decisions. In (a), (b), and (c) at least one party is not interested in the trade. In (d) both parties are interested in the trade and the trade takes place

Figure 9-1(b), illustrates the situation, where the general value of product B greater than the general value of product A for the trader. The trader is interested in the monetary value only. However, for the consumer, the general value of product A offered by the trader is lower than the general value of product B currently possessed by the consumer. Thus, the trader is willing to trade but the consumer is not. For this reason, the trade does not occur.

The situation shown in Figure 9-1(c) is the opposite to the situation in Figure 9-1(b). The monetary value of product B, which is equal to its general value for the trader is lower than the monetary value of the trader's product A and the trader is not interested in the trade. The consumer is willing the trade because the general value of product A is higher than the general value of product B for the consumer. The trade does not happen.

The situation shown in Figure 9-1(d), is the only situation, where both participants, the trader and the consumer are willing to trade. The general value (the monetary value only) of product B is higher than the general value (the monetary value only) of product A for the trader and the general value of product A is higher than the general value of product B for the consumer. The trade takes place. In result of this trade, both parties, the trader and the consumer, increase their general values.

9.3 Marginal Value for the Trader and the Consumer

In the trade situation shown in Figure 9-1(d), the trader has increased his monetary value by the difference in general values of two products, A and B, i.e. by the increment ΔVT

$$\Delta VT = VT_B - VT_A = VT_B^M - VT_A^M = \Delta VT^M \quad (9.5)$$

where ΔVT^M is the difference of monetary values of products, A and B,

$$\Delta VT^M = VT_B^M - VT_A^M > 0 \quad (9.6)$$

We refer to the increment ΔVT as the marginal value of the trade and ΔVT^M as to the marginal monetary value of the trade. The marginal general value for the trader is equal to the marginal monetary value, i.e. $\Delta VT = \Delta VT^M$ (Eq.(9.5)). Notice, that the trader and the consumer are both satisfied with the result of the trade because both have increased their general value. The consumer's marginal general value is

$$\Delta VC = VC_A - VC_B = VC_A^M + VC_A^N - VC_B^M - VC_B^N =$$
$$= VC_A^M - VT_B^M + VC_A^N - VC_B^M - VC_B^N = \quad (9.7)$$
$$= \Delta VC^M + \Delta VC^N > 0$$

where

$$\Delta VC^M = VC_A^M - VC_B^M; \quad \Delta VC^N = VC_A^N - VC_B^N \quad (9.8)$$

The rate of monetary value increment for the trader in this trade is

$$RVT^M = \frac{\Delta VT^M}{VT_A^M} = \frac{VT_B^M - VT_A^M}{VT_A^M} \quad (9.9)$$

9.4 The Chain of Barter Trades to Grow Monetary Value

The trader has increased his monetary value by margin ΔVT^M in one barter trade as schematically illustrated in Figure 9-1(d). Suppose the trader has performed a series of N sequential barter trades. In each trade k, the trader increased his monetary value by margin ΔVT_k^M for $k = 1, \ldots, N$,

$$\Delta VT_k^M = VT_{B,k}^M - VT_{A,k}^M \quad (9.10)$$

where $VT_{A,k}^M$ is the monetary value (equal to the general value) in the hands of the trader before trade k and $VT_{B,k}^M$ is the general value in hands of the consumer before trade k.

The total increase of the trader's monetary value in the chain of N trades is

$$\Delta VT_{Total}^M = \sum_{k=1}^{N} \Delta VT_k^M \quad (9.11)$$

The total rate of growth of the monetary value for the trader in this chain of barter trades, RVT_{Total}^M,

$$RVT_{Total}^M = \frac{\Delta VT_{Total}^M}{VT_A^M} = \frac{VT_{B,N}^M - VT_{A,1}^M}{VT_{A,1}^M} \qquad (9.12)$$

where $VT_{B,N}^M$ is the monetary value of the product in hands of the consumer before the last trade N, which became the final monetary value in hands of the trader after the last trade, while $VT_{A,1}^M$ is the monetary value in hands of the trader before he initiated the barter trading chain.

The total rate of growth of the monetary value for the trader in the chain of barter trades, RVT^M, can be expressed as

$$RVT_{Total}^M = \prod_{k=1}^{N}\left(RVT_k^M + 1\right) - 1 =$$
$$= \left[\left(RVT_1^M + 1\right)\left(RVT_2^M + 1\right)\cdots\left(RVT_N^M + 1\right)\right] - 1 \qquad (9.13)$$

The average monetary rate for each trade, if $ARVT^M$ is defined as

$$\left(ARVT^M + 1\right)^N = \prod_{k=1}^{N}\left(RVT_k^M + 1\right) \qquad (9.14)$$

or

$$ARVT^M = \left(\prod_{k=1}^{N}\left(RVT_k^M + 1\right)\right)^{1/N} - 1 \qquad (9.15)$$

Then according to Eqs.(9.15) and (9.13), the total rate of growth of the monetary value for the trader in this chain of the barter trades is

$$RVT_{Total}^M = \left(ARVT^M + 1\right)^N - 1 \qquad (9.16)$$

The initial monetary value in hands of the trader was VT_{Start}^M and the final monetary value in his hands after the completion of the chain of N barter trades was VT_{Final}^M,

$$VT_{Start}^M = VT_{A,1}^M \quad \text{and} \quad VT_{Final}^M = VT_{B,N}^M \qquad (9.17)$$

9 Trading a Paper Clip for a Single Family Home

The final monetary value in the hands of the trader after completion of N barter trades according to Eqs.(9.12) and (9.17) is

$$VT^M_{Final} = VT^M_{Start} \prod_{k=1}^{N}\left(1+RVT^M_k\right) = VT^M_{Start}\left(1+ARVT^M\right)^N$$

(9.18)

To grow the monetary value from VT^M_{Start} to VT^M_{Final} in N barter trades, the trader has to achieve the average monetary rate

$$ARVT^M = \exp\left(\frac{1}{N}\ln\left(\frac{VT^M_{Final}}{VT^M_{Start}}\right)\right) - 1$$

(9.19)

Thus, to grow the monetary value from VT^M_{Start} to VT^M_{Final} with the average marginal monetary rate for each trade, $ARVT^M$, the trader needs to perform N trades. This number can be calculated as

$$N = \frac{\ln\left(VT^M_{Final}/VT^M_{Start}\right)}{\ln\left(1+ARVT^M\right)}$$

(9.20)

9.5 From a Paper Clip to a Single-Family Home

Suppose the trader starts with a paper clip that has a monetary value of five cents – just a nickel. Also suppose that the trader can perform barter trades with average monetary trade rate $ARVT^M$. How many such average trades, N, does the trader need to perform to end up with a single-family home that costs $100,000? It means that the trader should grow his monetary value by $VT^M_{Final}/VT^M_{Start} = 2$ million times. The number of trades can be calculated according to Eq.(9.20).

Table 9-1 shows the number of barter trades needed to start with a paper clip (monetary value 5 cents) and end up with a single-family home (monetary value $100,000) in a chain of barter trades depending on the average trade rate.

Table 9-1: Number of barter trades needed to start with a paper clip (monetary value 5 cents) and end up with a single family home (monetary value $100,000) in a chain of barter trades

$ARVT^M$	10%	20%	30%	40%	50%
N (number of trades)	153	80	56	44	36

As is evident from Table 9-1, the trader needs 153 barter trades with 10% average trade rate in each trade. This number drops to 36 trades, if the trader manages to do the barter trade chain with the average rate 50% in each trade. Such a chain trade is quite doable, and for a well capable trader, the goal can be achieved in a reasonable number of barter trades.

Figure 9-2 shows the growth of the trader's monetary value, VT^M with the number of barter trades at a given average marginal growth rate, $ARTV$, when the trader starts with 5 cents and ends with $100,000. The higher average marginal rate, the lower number of trades is needed to achieve the goal.

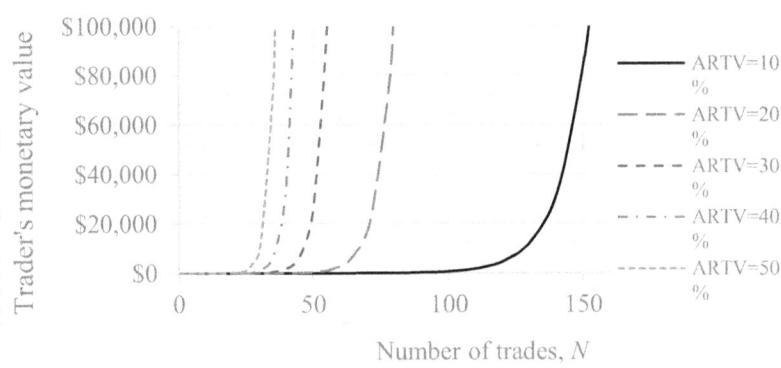

Figure 9-2: Dependence of the trader's monetary value VT^M on the number of barter trades at different average monetary growth rates, $ARTV^M$

The dependence of the number of barter trades for achieving the goal, VT^M_{Final} = $100,000, starting with VT^M_{Start} = 5 cents (i.e. grow the trader's monetary value by $VT^M_{Final} / VT^M_{Start}$ =

2 million times), on the average monetary growth rate, *ARTV*, is presented in Figure 9-3, explicitly showing that the number of the required trades is decreasing with the growth of the average monetary growth rate, $ARTV^M$.

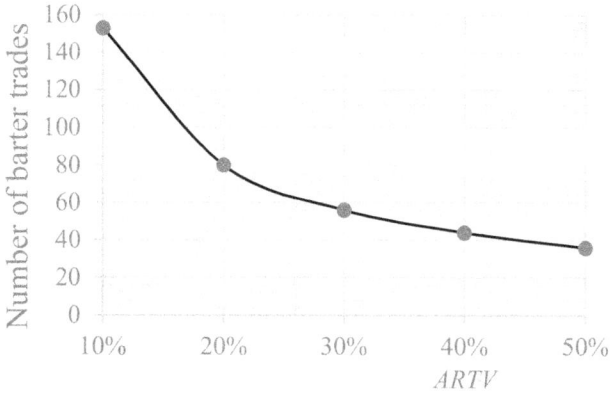

Figure 9-3: Dependence of the required number of trades, *N*, to grow the trader's monetary value in a barter trade chain by 2,000,000 times (from $VT^M_{Start} = \$0.05$ to $VT^M_{Final} = \$100,000$) on the average monetary growth rates, $ARTV^M$

As is evident from Figure 9-2, the trader's monetary value grows exponentially, showing a quite shallow growth in the beginning and rapid growth as the trade chain progresses, which is typical for the exponential function. It is important for the trader to maintain the monetary value growth rate in each trade. The higher the rate the faster the trader will reach the target monetary value.

9.6 Using Nonmonetary Value for Growing Monetary Profit

This chapter has described a chain of barter trades for the purpose of growing the trader's monetary value. The analysis was performed from the perspective of the theory of general value. General value is a combination of monetary and nonmonetary values. In each trade, the trader performed a barter trade with a consumer, possibly different in each trade. The trader was interested in the growth of the monetary value, while the consumer was interested in the growth of general value. Focusing on the monetary value, the trader can relatively quickly grow the monetary value. Thus, a chain of barter trades can grow the trader's monetary value from a very small initial amount to practically any target amount.

In each trade, the trader and the consumer increase their general value. This is a criterium for agreeing on the trade. The consumer trades with the goal of growing the general value, that included both, monetary and nonmonetary values. The trader, on the other hand, was trading for increasing his monetary value only. For this reason, both parties consider each trade to be fair. The consumer was satisfied with a trade, even giving up some monetary value but increasing the nonmonetary value above the loss in the monetary value, that resulted in the growth of the consumer general value. The trader, who was interested in the monetary value only, has increased his general value in each trade by the increment of the monetary value. A series of the targeted trades may result in a significant growth of the trader's monetary value.

In the example given in this paper, the trader started with a paper clip that costs 5 cents and in a series of chain trades, ended up with a single-family home with the monetary value of $100,000, i.e. has grown his monetary value by 2 million times in a reasonable number of barter trades.

Coming back to the case mentioned in the beginning of the paper, where Kyle MacDonald has traded a big Red paper clip into a house in Kipling Canada in 14 barter trades, we can assess this barter chain as the following. We have no actual data but may guess that the price for a big Red paper clip, as it was shown in the publication, was about $3 and a house in Kipling, Canada was about $10,000 at that time. Then according to Eq.(9.18), the trader should conduct the trades with the average monetary growth rate $ARTV^M = 84\%$ per trade to achieve the final result. Such a rate is quite high but reasonable for a good salesman, particularly, with all the excitement of this unusual experiment.

10 Competitive Strategy

10.1 General Value of Products to Purchase

The term product includes both, goods or services. The monetary component of value of product A, V_A^M, includes its price including cost of money, cost of maintenance, possibly, generated income by the product, and final utilization. The monetary value V_A^M may be represented by their amounts or by the perception of all associated amounts if they go beyond the normal neutral perception range for the consumer. The nonmonetary component of value of the product, V_A^N, represents the perception of the product itself by the consumer as the satisfaction from the product.

Let's for the sake of simplicity, consider only utility of price as the monetary value of the product. Extending this approach by adding cost of money, cost of maintenance, possibly, generated income by the product, and final utilization can be easily done, if needed, by simply adding these parameters to the monetary value of the product.

The price, P_A, of a consumer product contributes to the general value of the product with the negative sign because the amount paid for a consumer product reduces the amount of money in the possession of the buyer and consumer products are bought for consumption rather than for the resale. The monetary component of value can be measured in terms of utility of money, $U(P_A)$, for a given individual as

$$V_A^M = -U(P_A) \qquad (10.1)$$

The nonmonetary component of general value, V_A^N, of the same product A represents the level of satisfaction for the given consumer with the product regardless of its price. Thus, the general value of product A for a consumer is

$$V_A = -U(P_A) + V_A^N \qquad (10.2)$$

The utility of money may significantly differ from the amount of money, particularly, when the amount goes beyond the normal affordable range for the given individual. By the normal affordable range, we understand the amount of money, which do not cause any significant financial or psychological stress for the individual. In the normal range of affordable prices, the utility of money can be relatively accurately approximated just by the amount of money, i.e.

$$U(P_A) = P_A \qquad (10.3)$$

that makes the monetary value of the product equal the price of the product with the negative sign as

$$V_A^M = -P_A \qquad (10.4)$$

However, if the price goes beyond the normal affordable range, the difference between the amount and utility of money cannot be ignored.

10.2 Buying Decision without Additional Constrains

Consumers normally consider for purchasing those goods or services, which have positive general value for them. Consumers consider a product for purchasing, if the general value of the product in the perception of the consumer is positive, i.e.

the product's nonmonetary value is greater than the perception of its price according to Eq.(10.2). In other words, the consumer believes that the satisfaction obtained form the product is worth the price paid for it. An example of the positive general value for product A is shown in Figure 10-1(a). On the other hand, if the general value of a good or service is negative, as illustrated in Figure 10-1(b) for product B, the consumer does not consider buying the product because the consumer's satisfaction with the product is not worth the price.

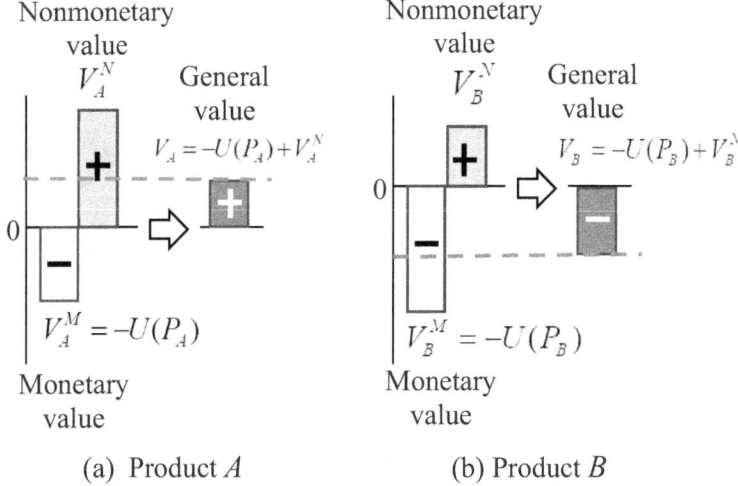

(a) Product A (b) Product B

Figure 10-1: An example of (a) the positive general value of product A that may lead to a buying decision by the consumer and (b) the negative general value of product B that leads to a not-buying decision by the consumer

Thus, consumers consider products with the positive general values and do not consider products with the negative general values.

In choosing between two competitive products with positive general values, the consumer prefers the product with the higher general value as illustrated in Figure 10-2.

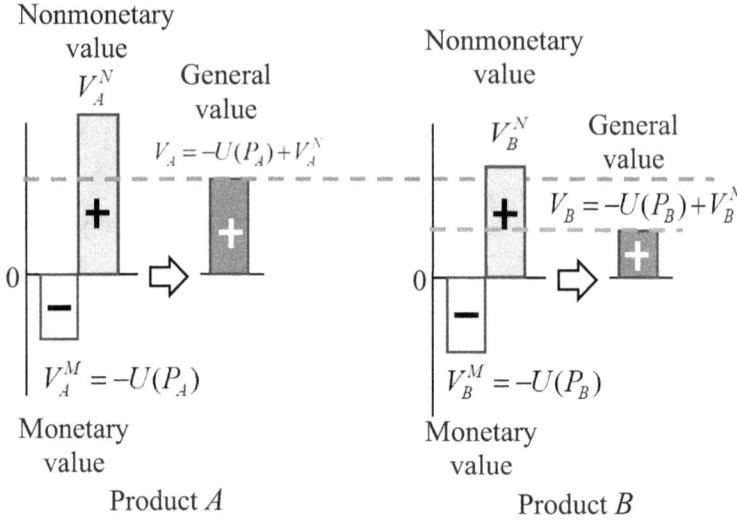

Figure 10-2: An example of the general value of product *A* higher than the general value of product *B* that makes the buyer prefer product *A*

The difference of the nonmonetary values of these products can be interpreted as the products differentiation. The relative nonmonetary value of two products, i.e. the difference of their nonmonetary values, can be measured by finding the indifference point for each consumer or a group of consumers as was discussed in Chapter 3.

Figure 10-3 shows two products, *A* and *B*, which offer the same general value tough their monetary and nonmonetary components are different. The higher price for product *B* is compensated by the higher nonmonetary value (satisfaction, differentiation, or need) of product *B* relative to product *A*, resulting in the equal general values of both products.

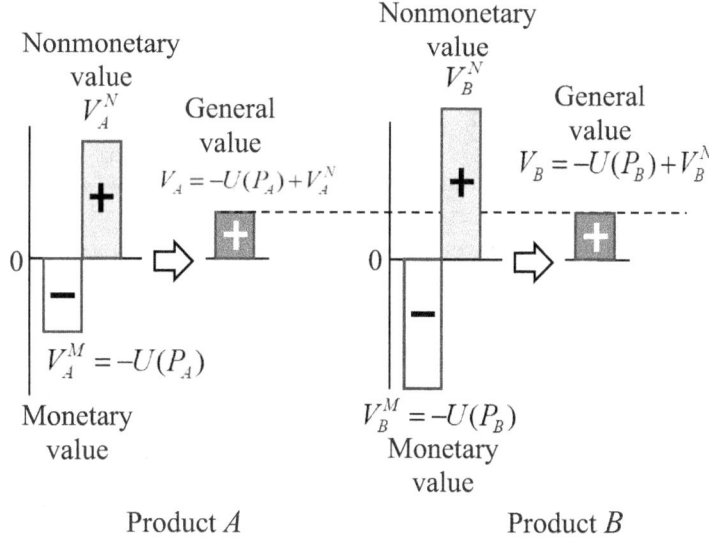

Figure 10-3: An example of the equal general values of products A and B for a specific consumer

Two products, which offer the same general value for the consumer as shown in Figure 10-3, are equally competitive in the market, if there are no additional constraints influencing the consumers buying decisions such as price constraints or differentiation constraints (quality, specific features, etc.). For example, product B in Figure 10-3 offers the higher differentiation (nonmonetary value) than product A, but, on the other hand, product B is more expensive than product A. However, in result, both products offer the same general values. Thus, the consumer should be indifferent about buying either product unless the consumers have certain constraints in their buying decision-making.

Nonmonetary values of products and services are specific for each consumer but possibly, similarly shared by a certain group of consumers. Thus, similar nonmonetary values can be referred to specific groups of consumers. For example, tastes and perception of the generation of millennials are significantly different from the tastes and perception of the generation of baby boomers, though are quite similar inside each generation group.

Typically, groups of consumers sharing similar interests and lifestyle are expected to share similar nonmonetary values.

10.3 Sales of Computer Monitors as an Example of Competitive Power

Currently outdated CRT computer monitors were the primary computer monitors on the market up to the end of the 20th century. Later, they were replaced by the flat panel monitors. Let's use this case for the competitive analysis of the monitors based on the assessment of their general values for consumers as illustrated in Figure 10-4.

It is obvious that flat panel monitors offer the higher nonmonetary value than CRT monitors due their convenience and, at the present time, quality of picture. For the sake of simplicity, let's use price as an amount of money to represent the product monetary value as it was discussed above.

Up to the late 1990s, flat panel monitors were extremely expensive compared to the matching CRTs that did not match the nonmonetary differentiation. For this reason, consumers were not interested in the flat panels and the CRTs were dominated the market. Flat panel monitors were not present in the consumer market at all because of their negative general value caused by the high price Figure 10-4(a)):

- General value of the CRTs was positive
- General value of flat panel monitors was negative.
- Flat panel monitors were not present in the consumer market.

In the late 1990s, production costs and hence, the price for the flat panel monitors dropped and their general value turned positive, though was still much lower than the general value of the CRTs (Figure 10-4(b)). During this period, flat panel monitors appeared in the consumers market but had a quite low market share:

- General value of the CRTs was positive
- Cost of flat panel monitors and price dropped (monetary value) and quality improved (nonmonetary value) that made general value of flat monitors positive but stll lower, than the general value of CRT monitors.

10 Competitive Strategy

	CRT Monitors	Flat Panel Monitors	Comments
Mid 1990s (a)	*[diagram: CRT monitor value chart showing nonmonetary value V_{CRT}^N, general value $V_{CRT} = -P_{CRT} + V_{CRT}^N$ (positive), and monetary value $V_{CRT}^M = -P_{CRT}$]*	*[diagram: Flat panel monitor value chart showing nonmonetary value V_{Flat}^N, general value $V_{Flat} = -P_{Flat} + V_{Flat}^N$ (negative), and monetary value $V_{Flat}^M = -P_{Flat}$]*	• General value of CRTs was positive • General value of flat panel monitors was negative. Flat panel monitors were not present in the consumer market.
Late 1990s (b)	*[diagram: CRT monitor value chart showing nonmonetary value V_{CRT}^N, general value $V_{CRT} = -P_{CRT} + V_{CRT}^N$ (positive), and monetary value $V_{CRT}^M = -P_{CRT}$]*	*[diagram: Flat panel monitor value chart showing nonmonetary value V_{Flat}^N, general value $V_{Flat} = -P_{Flat} + V_{Flat}^N$ (positive but smaller), and monetary value $V_{Flat}^M = -P_{Flat}$]*	• General value of CRTs was positive • Production cost of flat panel monitors and hence, their price reduced (monetary value) and quality improved (nonmonetary value) that made general value of flat monitors positive but still lower, than the general value of CRT monitors. Flat panel monitors appeared in the consumer market but weak in their competition with the CRT monitors.

Figure 10-4 (a,b): Competition between CRT and flat panel monitors from the perspective of general value

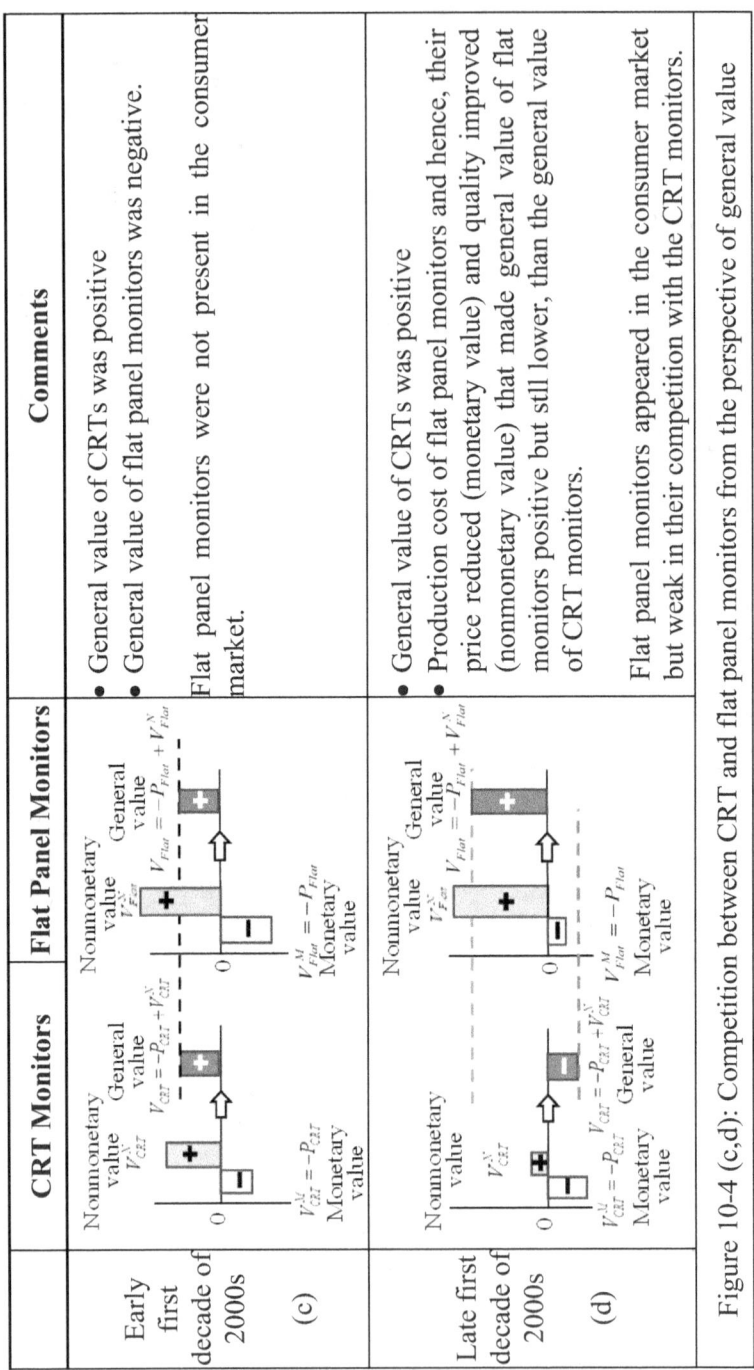

Figure 10-4 (c,d): Competition between CRT and flat panel monitors from the perspective of general value

10 Competitive Strategy

- Flat panel monitors appeared in the consumer market but weak in their competition with the CRT monitors.

At the turn of the century, the production costs and hence, prices for the flat panel monitors were significantly reduced to the degree, that general values of flat monitors and the CRTs equalized, thus, both types of monitors had almost the same general value (Figure 10-4(c)). In result, both types of monitors were equally competitive in the market in the early 2000s:

- General value of CRTs stayed positive though their nonmonetary value declined.
- Production cost of flat panel monitors and hence, their price reduced (monetary value increased), quality improved (nonmonetary value increased) that made general value of flat monitors positive and matching general value of CRT monitors.
- Both, flat panels and the CRTs equally competed in the cog

The progress in the flat panel monitors technology has led to a significant drop in the production cost and significant improvement in the quality of flat panel monitors. Thus, by the end of the first decade of the 21st century, the general value of flat panel monitors significantly increased, while general value of the CRTs had dropped as shown in Figure 10-4 (d). In result, CRT monitors had been washed out from the market:

- Nonmonetary value of CRTs significantly dropped making their general value negative.
- Production cost of flat panel monitors and price significantly dropped (monetary value) and quality improved (nonmonetary value) that brought general value of flat monitors much higher relative to the CRTs.
- In result, CRTs lost in the competition and washed out from the market.

The schematic analysis above has clearly and explicitly demonstrated a constructive approach of the concept of general value in competitive analysis. Among competing products, i.e., goods or services, products with the higher general value succeed in the competition. Products with the negative general values are forced to leave the market.

10.4 Buying Decisions under Monetary and Nonmonetary Constrains

Most consumers have certain constraints impacting their buying decisions. Such constraints could be monetary constraints, representing certain limitations on the affordable price or reservation price, as well as nonmonetary constraints, representing special requirements to the product quality, differentiation, etc.

Suppose three competing products, A, B, and C, are offering similar general values, though have different monetary and nonmonetary components of value as shown in Figure 10-5 and Figure 10-6. It looks that the all three products should equally share the market because they offer the same level of general value.

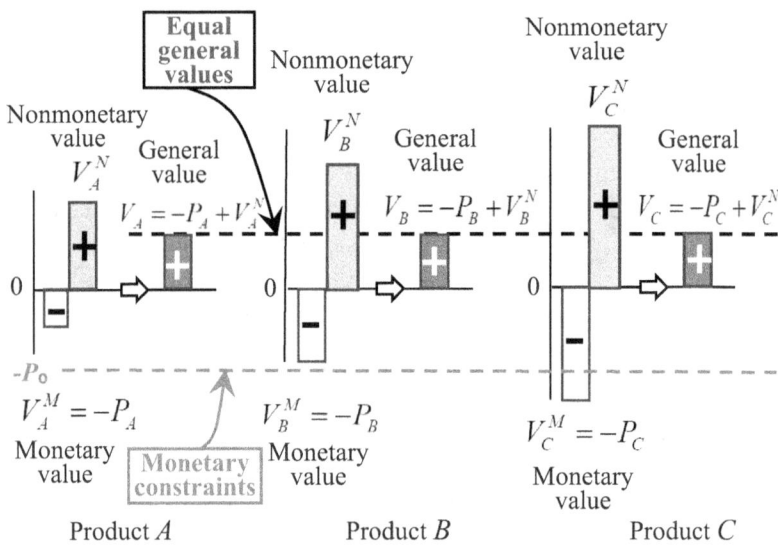

Figure 10-5: An example of equal general values offered by products A, B and C (the upper dotted line) superimposed with the monetary (price) consumer constraints (the lower dotted line) that pushes product C out of the market

However, some of the products with the same general value may have unaffordable prices or offer substandard features that mat reduce their competitive power. Some level of prices may

10 Competitive Strategy

be unaffordable for certain categories of consumers due to their income or other limitations, while some other consumers may have the lower reservation prices for those products. These limitations impose monetary constraints, say P_0. It means that the products with the price P, higher than price P_0, that represents the monetary constraint (the lower dotted line in Figure 10-5), i.e., the products with $P > P_0$, are not considered for purchasing by this category of consumers. As is clear from Figure 10-5, prices for products A and B are lower than the monetary constraint, i.e. $P_A < P_0$, and $P_B < P_0$, while the price for product C is higher than the monetary constraint, i.e., $P_C > P_0$. Thus, product C is not considered for purchasing regardless of its general value but due to monetary constraints. In result, only products A and B are successfully competing in the market, but product C becomes uncompetitive for this particular category of consumers.

As an example, one may compare generic and fashion cloths. Generic cloths have the lower price but offer the lower differentiation for the consumers. Some categories of consumers do not consider a high-end cloth for purchasing regardless of their fashion and quality due to monetary (price) constraints. Some other categories of consumers may impose monetary constraints simply as a reservation price, say, deciding that they would not pay more than, say, $100 for a pair of shoes, not because they cannot afford it, but just they do not believe that shoes should worth more.

On the other hand, some consumers prefer products of high level of quality and differentiation. One can express such a nonmonetary constraint in terms of the lowest level of the nonmonetary value, the consumer is willing to consider for purchasing as schematically shown in Figure 10-6. Three products A, B, and C with the same general value (the Black dotted line across the products on the level of general value) are presented in the figure, where the nonmonetary constraint is shown with the Green dotted line across the products. It means that products with the nonmonetary value below a certain level are not considered for purchasing by this category of consumers. In the case shown in Figure 10-6, products A and B offer nonmonetary values below the level of the nonmonetary constraint, and therefore are not considered for purchasing, but only product C is considered for purchasing as its nonmonetary value is above the nonmonetary constraint.

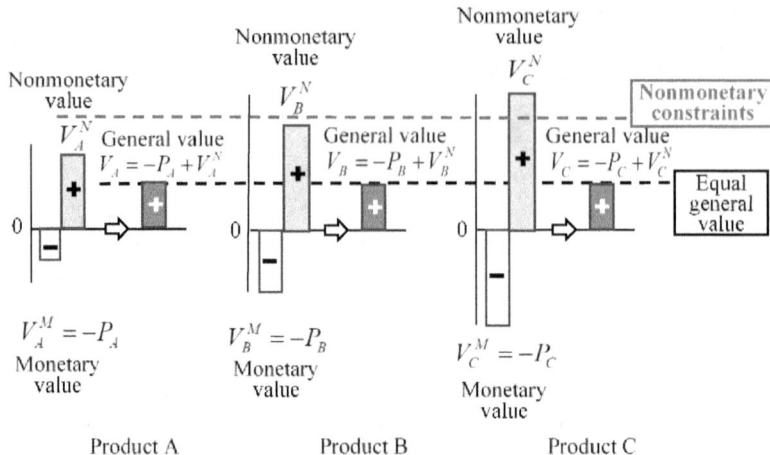

Figure 10-6: An example of the similar general values offered by products *A*, *B* and *C* (the lower dotted line) superimposed with the nonmonetary (quality, differentiation, etc.) consumer constraints (the upper dotted line) that pushes products *A* and *B* out of the market

As an example, a given category of consumers may consider only smart TV sets with the internet connection, not considering the TV sets, which have no such connection regardless of their prices.

Different monetary and nonmonetary constraints are imposed by different groups of consumers. Such constraints may relate to different groups of consumers and depend on income, taste, fashion, education, cultural values, habits, political situation, and many other factors.

11 Market Share Analysis

11.1 Analogy with Physics

Money in economics may play a similar role as energy in physics. (Ksenzhek, 2007; Aityan, 2011). We extend this analogy to the similarity between general value in economics and energy in physics. To go along with this analogy, it would be reasonable to assume that each transaction or action tends to bring an economic system to a state with the highest added value similarly to a trend of physical system to get to a state with the lowest potential energy in static equilibrium. If go beyond the monetary interpretation of value, the general value may play a similar role in economics as energy in physics where money or monetary utility is just one of the components of the "***economic energy***."

It may be the case that the current turmoil in global economy caused by certain lack and dissipation of economic energy on the global scale. This angle of view is yet to be pursued and analyzed.

11.2 Summarizing the Concept of General Value

The principle of increasing general value (Chapter 8) states that every action or transaction decision should lead to the increase of general value for every participant.

General value in economics plays a similar role as energy in physics. This analogy may be extended to the description and analysis of product market shares based on equilibrium controlled by general value. It would be reasonable to assume that each transaction or action tends to bring an economic system to a state with the highest added value similarly to the behavior of any physical system to get to a state with the lowest energy in equilibrium. Thus, we can refer to general value as *"economic energy"*.

11.3 Market Share Analysis as Boltzmann Distribution

Different competitive products may offer different general values for the consumers. It is reasonable to assume that among competitive products, the products with the higher general value, have the higher consumer demand. The question is, how these products would share the market. It is reasonable to assume that the product's general value plays the role of energy in the market. By analogy with the Boltzmann distribution in Physics, we can suggest that the demand for the competitive products would be exponentially distributed in the market based on their relative general values. This approach will be illustrated below, using two competitive products and then expanded to a variety of competitive products. For the sake of simplicity, we assume that there are no constraints imposed by the consumers.

11.3.1 Two Competitive Products without Consumer Constraints

Suppose there are only two different competitive products, present in the market, product 1 and product 2. The products offer general values V_1 and V_2 and the market shares of these products are C_1 and C_2. The market shares of the products represent the concentration of these products on the market, i.e. the balance of quantities of those products sold relative to the total sales of both product in the market. By analogy with the

Boltzmann distribution in Physics, the market shares of those products can be expressed as

$$\frac{C_1}{C_2} = \exp(\theta(V_1 - V_2)) = \exp(-\theta \Delta V_{12}) \qquad (11.1)$$

where ΔV_{12} is the difference of the general values of products 1 and 2

$$\Delta V_{12} = V_2 - V_1 \qquad (11.2)$$

and θ is the constant representing the degree of competition, liquidity, and other characteristics of the market in general.

The total marketshare of these two products is 1 (or 100%) representing the entire market for those products,

$$C_1 + C_2 = 1 \quad \text{where} \quad C_1 \geq 0; \; C_2 \geq 0 \qquad (11.3)$$

Thus, Eq.(11.1) can be rewritten as

$$\frac{C_1}{1 - C_1} = \exp(-\theta \Delta V_{12}) \qquad (11.4)$$

or

$$\frac{1 - C_2}{C_2} = \exp(-\theta \Delta V_{12}) \qquad (11.5)$$

and hence

$$\begin{aligned}
C_1 &= \frac{\exp(-\theta \Delta V_{12})}{\exp(-\theta \Delta V_{12}) + 1} = \frac{\exp(-\theta \Delta V_{12}/2)}{\exp(-\theta \Delta V_{12}) + \exp(-\theta \Delta V_{12})}; \\
C_2 &= \frac{1}{\exp(-\theta \Delta V_{12}) + 1} = \frac{\exp(-\theta \Delta V_{12}/2)}{\exp(\theta \Delta V_{12}/2) + \exp(-\theta \Delta V_{12}/2)}
\end{aligned} \qquad (11.6)$$

where C_1 and C_2 are varying from 0 (or 0%) to 1 (or 100%) of the market for those products.

It is worth to notice, that the market shares of the products depend on the difference of their general values rather than on the absolute level of each general value.

The market shares of products 1 and 2 as a function of the relative general value, ΔV_{12}, of product 1 versus product 2

(Eq.(11.2)) are shown in Figure 11-1. The relative general value of two products is referred to as the difference of general values of these two products. If both products have equal general values, they equally share the market 50%-50% ($C_1 = C_2 = \frac{1}{2}$). As the difference of their general values, $\Delta V_{12} = V_1 - V_2$, grows, product 1 is getting the greater market share tending to get the entire market, i.e. $C_1 \to 1$, if $\Delta V_{12} \to \infty$, i.e. grows indefinitely high. If the difference ΔV_{12} goes to the negative zone and keeps falling, $\Delta V_{12} \to -\infty$, the market share of product 1 becomes lower and tends falling to zero, i.e. $C_1 \to 0$.

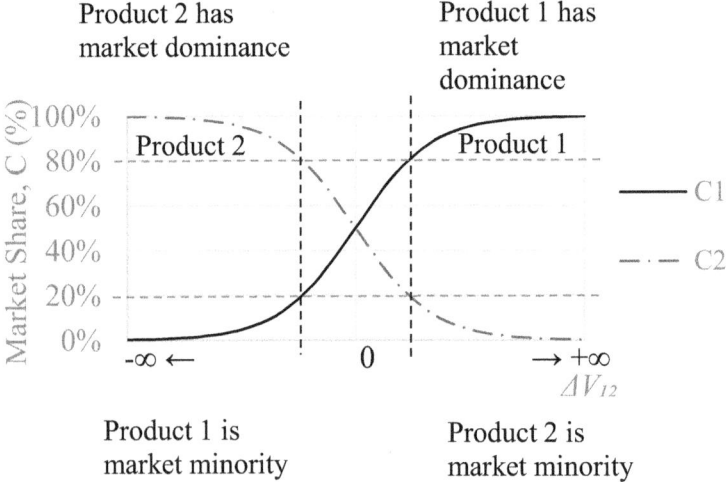

Figure 11-1: Distribution of product market shares of two competitive products as a function of the difference in their general values (solid curve for product 1 and dotted curve for product 2)

If the market share of a product rises above a certain level, the product becomes a dominant product in the market and may drive the competitive products off the market. On the other hand, if the market share of a product fall below a certain level, the product becomes a minority product and may fail in the market. Such dominance and minority levels are schematically shown in Figure 11-1. The dominance and minority levels of relative general values depend on the product, market, number of competitors, industry, degree of competition, access to inputs, and many other market defining parameters. The levels market share of 20% and 80% for minority products and dominant products are chosen arbitrary and used in this figure just for illustration.

Product positioning of dominant or majority products on the market, may dramatically impact on the business strategies of the companies producing those products.

11.3.2 Many Competitive Products without Consumer Constraints

Let's generalize the approach developed above for two competing products to many competing products. Suppose there are a variety of N different competitive products presented in the market. Each product offers a certain general value $V_1, V_2, \ldots V_N$. Suppose V_0 is a commonly accepted benchmark general value for these group of products in the market. Then the market shares of these products could be expressed as

$$C_k = \frac{\exp(\theta \Delta V_k)}{\sum_{k=1}^{N} \exp(\theta \Delta V_k)} \quad \text{for } k = 1, 2, \ldots, N \quad (11.7)$$

where ΔV_k is the difference of the general value of product k, V_k, and the benchmark general value, V_0, i.e.

$$\Delta V_k = V_k - V_0 \quad (11.8)$$

and the sum of all market values of all competing products makes 100%, i.e. makes the entire market for that category of products,

$$\sum_{k=1}^{N} C_k = 1 \quad (11.9)$$

Figure 11-2 shows a schematic distribution of product market shares of four competitive products as a function of the relative general value of product 1 versus the benchmark general value, $\Delta V_1 = V_1 - V_0$ while other relative general values, $\Delta V_k = V_k - V_0$ for $k = 2, 3,$ and 4 were held unchanged.

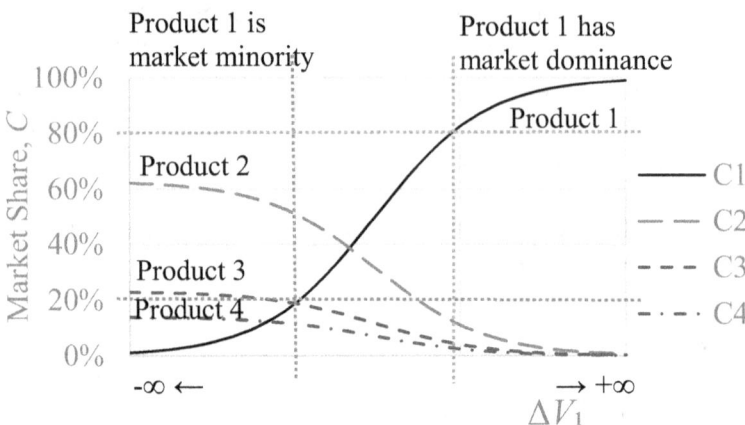

Figure 11-2: Distribution of product market shares of four competitive products as a function of the relative general value of product 1 versus the benchmark general value, V_1, while other relative general values are held unchanged

It is important to note that the benchmark general value V_o does not impact on the distribution of market shares of the products and plays a role of the reference point only. As soon as V_o is equally present in the exponents in both, nominator and denominator in Eq.(11.7), the actual value of the benchmark general value, V_o, does not play any role. The only significant role in the distribution of the product market shares is played by their relative general values.

As is evident from Figure 11-2, product 1 has extremely low market share if its relative general value is much lower relative to the other products and the product market share grows to the dominance level as its relative general value grows. On the other hand, other products gradually losing their market shares as the relative general value of product 1 grows.

Thus, the application of the Boltzmann distribution approach to the competitive analysis in the markets allows for the quantitative assessment of the competitive products and their market shares. The general values of the products play a role in the markets similar to energy in Physics.

11.4 Conclusions on Market Share

General value is a sum of monetary and nonmonetary values. In this chapter, we analyzed market shares of competitive products based on their general values. Competitive products may have different monetary and nonmonetary components of value. Monetary value relates to the consumer perception of the product price and possibly, maintenance and final disposal. Nonmonetary value relates to the consumer perception of the product, product differentiation, quality, and other parameters impacting on the consumer satisfaction. The product price, cost of maintenance and possibly, final disposal contribute to the monetary value with the negative sign because these amounts leave the consumer's pocket, while nonmonetary value contributes the general value with the positive sign.

Different products may offer similar general values while show different monetary and nonmonetary components of value. If one product offers a low price and a low nonmonetary value but another product has the higher price and the higher nonmonetary value, their general values may be equal due to the balance of the monetary and nonmonetary components of value.

Consumers make their buying decisions based on the general value of the product, unless there are certain constraints on monetary or nonmonetary values. Thus, products compete by offering the higher general value.

If a firm pursues the cost leadership competitive strategy, the firm needs to reduce production costs but try to keep the nonmonetary value of its products at least closer to the level of its competitors to offer the highest possible general value offered by its product due to its low cost and hence, the price. On the other hand, if a firm pursues the differentiation strategy, the firm needs increase the product differentiation, but try to control their product price not to grow too high to compromise the product high general value. If a firm manages to pursue both, cost and differentiation leadership, the firm's competitors may be washed out from the market due to unmatching differences in the general values of their products.

The difference in general values of the competitive products impacts on the market share of the respective products. The higher difference of general values of the products, the greater is the difference in their market shares. The market shares of the competitive products exponentially depend on the difference of their general values. The exponential distribution of the market shares of competitive products on their general values is similar to the Boltzmann distribution in Physics, where general value of the products metaphorically plays the role of energy in Physics.

Consumer constraints such as monetary and nonmonetary constraints may change the market shares of the products due to the elimination of the products, which do not meet the constraint.

Thus, the assessment based on general value allows for quantitative approach to competitive analysis with the estimation of the market shares of the competitive products.

12 Explanatory and Predictive Power of General Value

12.1 A Brief Summary of the Theory of General Value

The theory of general value provides a quantitative approach to the theory of value by separating the monetary and nonmonetary components of value. The nonmonetary component of value accounts for psychological factors and biases in contrast to the monetary component in trading and decision making. General value is represented as a linear combination of the monetary and nonmonetary components. Such an approach distinctly differs from the neoclassical utility and the decision variable in behavioral economics, where psicholical and monetary factors were considered jointly.

The monetary component of value (or monetary value) can be represented by the utility of money or by just the amount of money if the amount of money fits within the neutral perception for the given individual. The nonmonetary component of value (or nonmonetary value) is measured in the same units as the monetary component.

The nonmonetary value can be measured by finding the indifference point in making choices. At the indifference point, both choices offer the same general value, hence, the difference in monetary values of those choices is equal to the difference in nonmonetary values with the opposite sign.

12.2 The Explanatory Power of the Theory of General Value

The separation of monetary and nonmonetary components of value allows for a clear and measurable account for nonmonetary factors in decision making. Nonmonetary factors may go far beyond economic incentives and account for all psychological factors and biases, which can be distinctly measured, analyzed, amnd taken into account. The driving force and the goal of any decision making is maximization of general value.

12.2.1 Job Selection

In the selection of jobs or other professional engagements, individuals maximize their general value as a combination of monetary and nonmonetary values. Some individuals may focus mostly on the expected compensation, i.e. consider mostly monetary component of the general value. Some other individuals may choose jobs with lower monetary compensation if there are certain additional job incentives including healthcare support, better work conditions, proximity to home, or some other incentives. Some individuals may choose a job with the significantly lower monetary compensation (monetary value) if they like the work engagement and that professional activity itself. Regardless of the final choice, the decision depends on the maximization of the total general value offered by the job rather than just the monetary compensation. The relative nonmonetary value of a job against another job can be measured by reaching the indifference point when the individual is indifferent about accepting the offered jobs though these two jobs offer different monetary compensation.

12.2.2 Buying Decision for Consumer Products

Buying decisions of consumer products also depend on the general value of the product that includes the price with the negative sign as the monetary value and the nonmonetary value that comprises all psychological factors including the need in the product, convenience of the buying process, expected satisfaction with the product, its brand, psychological biases and anchors. The price contributes the general value of the consumer product with the negative sign because the product is being purchased for the consumption rather than for the resale.

Consumers are buying the products with the higher general value if there are no specific constraints. Specific monetary and nonmonetary constraints could be applied in the maximization of general value to influence buying decisions.

12.2.3 Resellers versus Consumers

Resellers and consumers both follow the general value maximization principle in their decision making. However, resellers focus mostly on the monetary value of the traded products while consumers consider both monetary and nonmonetary values. Such a difference in value assessment makes trading conducted by a reseller and a consumer quite different by its opportunities and final goals. A reseller's goal is to maximize the monetary value and a consumer's goal is to maximize the consumed (nonmonetary) value by minimizing the expenses (monetary value).

12.2.4 Market Competition

Products compete in the market by their value proposition to the consumers. Typically, the company competitive strategy could be based either on cost or differentiation. By keeping the costs low or reducing costs, the company can sell the products at the price lower than its competitors can. On the other hand, the product can offer specific differentiation compared to the competitive products and, for this reason sold at a premium price. Two typical questions often addressed in marketing and often asked to business students are:

- Can a company compete by both cost and differentiation?
- What is the balance between cost and differentiation?

The above questions are quite confusing for the traditional economic theories because they do not provide quantitative and measurable approach to analyze and compare values offered by the competitive products. The theory of general value can answer these questions by providing quantitative analysis of monetary and nonmonetary values of competitive products. The products that offer the same level of their general values stay equally competitive in the market regardless of the combination of monetary and nonmonetary components of value. Thus, competitive products sold by different prices and showing different levels of differentiation may equally compete in the market if they offer comparable general values. However, if a product leads by general value, i.e. by both monetary and nonmonetary values, then such a product defeats the competing products.

12.3 The Principal Strategic Goal of a Company

It is well known in the traditional economics (economic theories preceding the theory of general value) that the principal strategic goal of any for-profit company is maximization of its net present value, where value is considered in its traditional monetary meaning. However, formulation of the principal strategic goal of not-for-profit organizations typically ends up with the general statements about social values not based on any measurable quantities. The most confusing situation in the traditional economic theories occurs in an attempt to explain why many for-profit companies are involved in charity activities. Any donation for charity reduces the monetary value of the company, which is against the principal strategic goal. Something is wrong. Either companies involved in charity activity act against the theory, or maybe, something is wrong with the theory itself.

The theory of general value clearly and explicitly resolves this confusion by extending the principal strategic goal of any company to the maximization of net present general value that includes both monetary and nonmonetary components of value. The pure for-profit companies tend to maximize their general value, in which the major weight belongs to the monetary component. The not-for-profit companies also tend to maximize their general value, giving the major weight to the nonmonetary components of value. The for-profit companies involved in charitable activities, do reduce their monetary component of general value but increase the nonmonetary component of general values, maximizing their net present general value by compensating some loss of monetary value by the increase of the nonmonetary value.

12.4 Market Share Analysis and Prediction

Various products share markets offering different general values. Accurate analysis of the competitive power and correct prediction of the market share of the existing or new products offered in the market play a key role in handling competition and achieving commercial success. Products compete by their general value. The higher the product's general value relative to the competitive products, the greater its market share. Proceeding from the analogy of general value in economics with energy in physics, one can apply the Boltzmann distribution for the description of product market shares based on their general value. According to the Boltzmann distribution, market share of products can be described similar to the concentration of particles according to their energies in Physics. Such an approach provides a quantitative, measurable, and controllable tool for proper understanding, management, control, and prediction of product success in the competitive markets.

12.5 Cross-Industry Capital Flows Analysis and Prediction

Capital flows migrate from a less potential to a most potential markets and industries with the higher expected return on investment. Such a dynamics of capital flows can be explained and predicted by the difference of general values between the industries and markets. The intensity of capital flows depends on the specifics of the liquidity in the industries and cross-industry

Bibliography

Aityan, Sergey K. (2011). Price-Value Potential for Near-Perfectly Competitive Markets, *American Journal of Economics and Business Administration*, vol. 3 (4), p. 623–635.

Aityan, Sergey K. (2013). The Notion of General Value in Economics, *International Journal of Economics and Finance*, vol. 5, No. 5, pp. 1-14. ISSN:1576-2270, doi:10.5539/ijef.v5n5p1, http://www.ccsenet.org/journal/index.php/ijef/article/view/26698

Aityan, Sergey K.; Alexey K Ivanov-Schitz, and Shakar Thapa (2016) Measuring the Nonmonetary Component of General Value of Jobs, *Advances in Social Sciences Research Journal*, vol. 3, No. 12, pp. 1-33. doi:10.14738/assrj.312.2414, http://scholarpublishing.org/index.php/ASSRJ/article/view/2414/1516

Aityan, Sergey K.; Alexey K Ivanov-Schitz, and Eugenia Logunova (2017). Measuring the Nonmonetary Component of General Value for Goods and Services, *International Journal of Economics and Financial Issues*, vol. 7, No. 3, pp. 69-81. ISSN: 2146-4138, http: www.econjournals.com

Aityan, Sergey K. (2020 a). Analysis of Competitive Strategies by Asserting General Value, *International Journal of Economics and Finance*, vol. 12, No. 5, pp. 10-21.
doi:10.5539/ijef.v1 2 n 5 p 10

Aityan, Sergey K. (2020 b). A Barter Trade Chain—from a Paper Clip to a Single-Family House: A View from General Value, *Business and Economics Journal*, vol. 11, No. 3, pp. 1-6.
doi: 10.37421/2151-6219.2020.11.403

Becker, Gary (1968), Crime and Punishment: An Economic Approach, *The Journal of Political Economy*, vol.76, No. 2, pp.169–217. Mode of access: http://www.jstor.org/discover/10.2307/1830482?sid=21106242972313&uid=4&uid=2&uid=3738936

Becker, Gary S. and Kevin M. Murphy (2003). *Social Economics: Market Behavior in a Social Environment*, Harvard University Press, 190 pages.

Bergson, Abram (1938). A Reformulation of Certain Aspects of Welfare Economics, *Quarterly Journal of Economics*, vol. 52 (2), p. 310-334.

Bergson Abram (1954). On the concept of social welfare, *Quarterly Journal of Economics*, vol. 68, p. 233–252.

Bernoulli, Daniel (1738). Reprinted in 1954, Exposition of a New Theory on the Measurement of Risk, *Econometrica (The Econometric Society)*, vol. 22 (1), p. 22–36, http://www.jstor.org/stable/1909829

Bertrand, J. (1883) "Book review of theoriemathematique de la richesse sociale and of recherches sur les principles mathematiques de la theorie des richesses", *Journal de Savants*, vol. 67, pp. 499–508.

Bilo, Simon (2005). *Imputation and Value in the Works of Menger, Böhm-Bawerik and Wieser*, The Ludwig von Mises Institute, http://nb.vse.cz/kfil/elogos/miscellany/bilo105.pdf.

Blackaby, D. H. and P. D. Murphy (1995), Earnings, Unemployment and Britain's North-South Divide: Real or Imaginary?, *Oxford Bulletin of Economics and Statistics*, Vol. 4, pp. 487–512. Mode of access: http://onlinelibrary.wiley.com/doi/10.1111/j.1468-0084.1995.tb00036.x/pdf

Böhm-Bawerk, Eugen (1890). *Capital and Interest: A Critical History of Economical Theory*, London: Macmillan, (first published in 1884)

Brown, Charles. (1980). Equalizing Differences in the Labor Market, *Quarterly Journal of Economics*, vol. 94 (1), p. 113-134.

Chipman, John S. and James C. Moore (1980). Compensating Variation, Consumer's Surplus, and Welfare, *American Economic Review*, vol. 70 (5), p. 933-949.

Coase, Ronald (1937). The Nature of the Firm, *Economica*, vol. 4 (16), p. 386–405.

Friedman, Milton and L. J. Savage (1948). The Utility Analysis of Choices Involving Risk, *Journal of Political Economy*, 56 (4): 279–304.

Friedman, Milton (1953). *Essays in Positive Economics*. Chicago: University of Chicago Press, 329 p.

From paper-clip to house in 14 trades (July 7, 2006). CBC News, https://www.cbc.ca/news/canada/from-paper-clip-to-house-in-14-trades-1.573973

Gale, Bradley T. and Donald J. Swire (2006). Value-Based Marketing & Pricing, *Working Paper of Customer Value, Inc.*, p. 1-19, http://www.cval.com/pdfs/VBMarketingAndPricing.pdf

Hacking, Ian (1980). Strange Expectations, *Philosophy of Science*, vol. 47, p. 562-567.

Gossen, Hermann H. (1854), Die Entwickelung der Gesetze des menschlichen Verkehrs, und der darausfließenden Regelnfürmenschliches Handeln. In English: The Laws of Human Relations and the Rules of Human Action Derived Therefrom (1983), MIT Press, ISBN 0-262-07090-1

Han, Seungjin and Shintaro Yamaguchi (2015), Compensating wage differentials in stable job matching equilibrium, *Journal of Economic Behavior & Organization*, Elsevier, vol. 114(C), pages 36-45

Hicks, John R. (1939). *Value and Capital: An Inquiry into some Fundamental Principles of Economic Theory*, Oxford, Clarendon Press.

Hollander Samuel (1979). *The Economics of David Ricardo*, Heinemann Educational Publishers, 774 p.

Jevons, William (1879). *The Theory of Political Economy*, Republished by Kessinger Publishing (2010), 343 p.

Kahn, Alfred E. (1979). Applications of Economics to an Imperfect World, *American Economic Review*, vol. 69 (2), p. 1–13.

Kahneman, Daniel and Amos Tversky (1979), Prospect Theory: An Analysis of Decision Under Risk, *Econometrica*, vol. 47, No. 2, pp. 263-291

Kahneman, Daniel, Paul Slovic, and Amos Tversky (1982). *Judgment under Uncertainty: Heuristics and Biases*, Cambridge: Cambridge University Press, 544p.

Kahneman, Daniel and Amos Tversky (2000). *Choices, Values, and Frames*, Cambridge University Press, 860 p.

Kahneman, Daniel (2011). *Thinking, Fast and Slow*, Farrar, Straus and Giroux, 512 p.

Kreps, David; Jose Scheinkman (1983). Quantity Precommitment and Bertrand Competition Yield

Cournot Outcomes, *Bell Journal of Economics*, vol. 14, pp. 326-338.

Ksenzhek, Octavian. (2007). *Money: Virtual Energy: Economy Through the Prism of Thermodynamics*, Universal Publishers, 212 p.

Lucas, Robert (1988). On the Mechanics of Economic Development, *Journal of Monetary Economics*, vol. 22 (1), p. 3–42.

Man Turns Paper Clip into House (July 11, 2006), BBC News, http://news.bbc.co.uk/2/hi/technology/5167388.stm

Marshall, Alfred (1890), *Principles of Economics*, London: Macmillan and Co., Ltd

Martin, Robert (2011). The St. Petersburg Paradox, *The Stanford Encyclopedia of Philosophy,* (Winter 2011 Edition), Edward N. Zalta (ed.), http://plato.stanford.edu/archives/win2011/entries/paradox-stpetersburg/.

Marx, Karl (1867). *Das Kapital. Kritik der politischenOekonomie*, Vertag von Otto Meissner, Reprinted by Penguin Classics (1992), vol. 1, 1152 p.; (1993) vol. 2, 624 p.; (1993) vol. 3, 1152 p.

McKenzie, Richard B. and Gordon Tullock (1981). *The New World of Economics: Explorations into the Human Experience*. New York: Irwin, Chaps. 2, 20.

Menger, Carl (2007), *Principles of Economics*, CreateSpace. (Original work published in 1871)

von Mises, Ludwig (2012). *The Theory of Money and Credit*, Reprinted by Snowball Publishing, 274 p. (Original work published in 1912)

Murphy, Robert P. (2011). *The Chicago School versus the Austrian School*, Ludvig von Mises Intitute, http://mises.org/daily/5390/The-Chicago-School-versus-the-Austrian-School.

von Neumann, John & Oskar Morgenstern (1944). *Theory of Games and Economic Behavior*. Princeton, NJ: Princeton University Press.

Pareto, Vilfredo (1906). *Manuale di Economia Politics, con una IntroduzioneullaScienzaSociale*, SocietaEditriceLibraria.

Peterson, Craig H. and W. Chris Lewis (1998). *Managerial Economics*, Prentice Hall, Fourth Edition, 672 p.

Pollis, Adamantia and Bertram L. Koslin (1962). On the Scientific Foundations of Marginalism, *American*

Journal Of Economics & Sociology, vol. 21 (2), p. 113-130.

Ricardo, David (1817). *The Principles of Political Economy and Taxation*, Republished by Dover Publications (2004), 320 p.

Rhoads, Steven E. (2007). *Concise Encyclopedia of Economics* (*Marginalism*), Liberty Fund, Inc., David R. Henderson (editor), 656 p.

Rosen, Sherwin (1974). Hedonic Prices and Implicit Markets: Product Differentiation in Pure Competition, *Journal of Political Economy*. vol. 82 (1), p. 34-55.

Rosen, Sherwin (1986). The theory of equalizing differences, *Handbook of Labor Economics*, Chapter 12, vol 1, p. 641 – 692.

Samuelson, Paul (1938). A Note on the Pure Theory of Consumers' Behaviour. *Economica*, vol. 5, pp. 61-71.

Samuelson, Paul A. and William D. Nordhaus (2004), *Economics*, McGraw-Hill, ISBN 0-07-287205-5

Schulak, Eugen M. and Herbert Unterköfler (2011). *Austrian School of Economics*, Ludwig von Mises Institute.

Simon, Herbert A. (1955). A Behavioral Model of Rational Choice, *Quarterly Journal of Economics*, vol. 69, p. 99-118.

Simon, Herbert A. (1972), *Theories of Bounded Rationality*, North Holland Publishing company, pp. 161-176. Mode of access: http://mx.nthu.edu.tw/~cshwang/teaching-economics/econ5005/Papers/Simon-H=Theoriesof%20Bounded%20Rationality.pdf

Skousen, Mark (2005). *Vienna & Chicago, Friends or Foes?: A Tale of Two Schools of Free-Market Economics*, Capital Press, 306 p.

Smith, Adam (1776). *The Wealth of Nations*, Republished by Simon & Brown (2012), 482 p.

Stigler, George Joseph (1950a). The Development of Utility Theory, I, *Journal of Political Economy*, vol. 58 (4), p. 307-327.

Stigler, George Joseph (1950b). The Development of Utility Theory, II, *Journal of Political Economy*, vol. 58 (5), p. 373-396.

Strotz, Robert (1953). Cardinal utility, *American economic review*, vol. 43 (2), p. 384-397.

Walras, Leon (1874, 1877). *Elements of Pure Economics*, Reprinted by Routledge (2010) 620 p.
Wicksteed, Philip Henry (1910). *The Common Sense of Political Economy*, Book 1, Chapter 2 and elsewhere.
von Wieser, Friedrich (1889a), *Der Natürliche Wert*, Wien, Hoelder.
von Wieser, Friedrich (2012), Natural Value, (W Smart, Ed., & C. A. Malloch, Trans.). (Original work published 1889)

www.ingramcontent.com/pod-product-compliance
Lightning Source LLC
Chambersburg PA
CBHW071402210526
45465CB00001B/212